Psychic Living

Psychic Living

Tap into Your
Psychic Potential

ANDREI RIDGEWAY

Kensington Books
http://www.kensingtonbooks.com

KENSINGTON BOOKS are published by

Kensington Publishing Corp.
850 Third Avenue
New York, NY 10022

ISBN 1-57566-415-1

First Printing: July, 1999
10 9 8 7 6 5 4 3 2 1

Printed in the United States of America

Acknowledgments

This book came together with the support and encouragement of a whole clan of people. I express deep gratitude to my wife, Raïna Paris, for her meticulous inspection of each chapter, and for her wit, passion, and steadfast love; to my mother, Elizabeth Ridgeway, for introducing me to the psychic arts and teaching me how to breathe in the sacred worlds; to my agent, Laura Dail, for having faith in me as a young writer and giving her precious time and energy to examine my work; to my editor, Tracy Bernstein, for her sterling analysis of the final manuscript and her patient attendance with all my questions; to Corinne Lorain, owner of Caffe Luna, for allowing me to give Tarot readings to her customers and broaden my knowledge of the human race; to my sister, Gigi Ridgeway, for reading the chapter on dreams and helping me stay in tune with all that is unseen; to George Hertzberg, for his clever advice on the opening chapters and his Monty Python humor; to Wesley Idol III, for his suggestions on the warrior section and his compassionate ear; to John Butler, for his philosophical critique and poignant honesty; to my brother, George Ridgeway, for teaching me a method of hands-on prediction and inspiring me to write from the heart; to Loren Beck, for his bull's-eye commentary and magical touch; to Teresa De Gracia, for attempting to edit the empath section with me after a bottle of red wine; to Lorin Roche and his wife, Camille Maurine, for reminding me there are no limits to the human soul; to Odette Springer, for being an artistic compatriot and a loving guide; to Reverend Carol, my spiritual mentor, for teaching me how to stay present in my body and let my soul do its thing; and finally, to all my clients, far and wide, who have allowed me the privilege of reading their lives and learning so very, very much.

Contents

PART I

Jewels of the Past

The Psychic Artist

Being inside human beings is where God learns.
　　　　　　　　　　　　　　—RILKE

 Before the advent of modern technology, before the invention of road signs and compasses, all human beings had to rely on was their instinct. If they needed to find new herbs for a cure, they would allow themselves to be directed through the forest to the appropriate source. On a hunt, they would follow the impulses that arose in their bodies, the subtle messages that led them to their prey. Each situation called for a different response. In order to survive, you had to be alert moment by moment to the voices that guided you. There were no news stations to prepare you for the arrival of a hurricane or a plague. Intuition was what kept you alive.

Nowadays, instead of responding to life instinctually, through the body, we have machines that do the feeling for us. With the influx of televisions, computers, and video games, many of our psychic skills are no longer called upon, and have drifted back into the subconscious. In most primitive cultures, powers such as telepathy and astral projection were as common in everyday life as verbal communication is today. Now these talents have become obsolete. Many of us consider this to be a product of evolution, but when you look beyond our fancy inventions and into the heart of modern culture, it is obvious that something great has been lost.

Since our psychic attributes have deteriorated, so has our ability to make balanced and healthy decisions concerning the welfare of our planet. The psychic sees the whole picture. Now that this part of us has been dismantled, we have become as dangerous as our machines.

Of course, I am not suggesting we give up our modern conveniences, our toilets and our telephones, and move back to the wilderness. But it is crucial to the survival of our species that we restore the intuitive gifts with which nature has endowed us, so that we can get back on track and fix our mistakes before it is too late.

As we are learning—through physics and other evolved sciences—everything in nature is interconnected. Just as the Taoist philosophers believed three thousand years ago, the cosmos is more like an organism than a machine. When we open ourselves to our psychic ability, we are immediately drawn to a way of life that complements the whole. This is what I call the "soul's path." When we find this groove, we are carried through the chaos gracefully. Taking the time to develop these powers can help prevent a great deal of suffering. It makes the ride smoother, the lessons more concrete.

When I was in Los Angeles during the 1994 earthquake, the first thing many people did once their house stopped shaking was to turn on their television to confirm the event. They needed CNN to tell them what had happened. The impulse was in all of us. Somewhere along the way, the media had become our psychic.

This book will help you restore your instincts, rewire your antennae so that you don't have to rely on external sources to tell you who you are and where you are going. In the end, we all must become our own guru, our own psychic, our own guardian angel. We can listen to messages from other people, but eventually we must learn to trust ourselves. This is something we all have in common.

Most people think of psychic power as a supernatural talent that only a few people possess, something otherworldly and mysterious. From years of psychic work, I have come to perceive it as something entirely different. The psychic in us is our animal nature that centuries of civilization has covered over. When we revive this part of us, it appears in our life with the same seamless grace as the migratory instinct of a wild bird. It feels natural and comfortable, like a well-fitting garment, adding to our character a confidence and ease that the intellect alone cannot provide.

Our intuitive nature connects us to the earth, gives us a feeling of purpose and intimacy with other human beings. We suddenly understand why we have chosen certain friends, why we enjoy a particular coffee shop so much, why we have a desire to sell our car and go on a meditation retreat to Tibet.

Although it enables us to feel closer to the stars, awakening our psychic ability is actually the most grounding and stabilizing thing we can do for ourselves, making our lives more real and purposeful than ever before. When we are in tune with this part of us, the most ordinary events take on profound meaning. Our life becomes a mythic adventure. We don't need drugs or alcohol to enhance our senses. Just being alive is enough.

When I began this career, I believed that the future was a fixed event and that we had no choice but to experience life the way it was planned for us by the gods. But after giving readings to thousands of people, I realized this wasn't true. People were not falling into the hands of some mysterious fate. They were each responsible for their own condition. The only help I could give them was to make them aware of the life they were creating so that they could change the direction of where they were going . . . that is, if they wanted to.

Becoming psychically attuned is a life's work and happens in stages. It begins with the development of our psychic instincts, various mind and body senses that make us receptive to divine guidance. Once these faculties are awakened, we begin making decisions that are in harmony with our soul's path, that bring our deepest dreams into action. Before we are hooked up to these instincts, it is very likely that we won't even know what we want to do with our lives. We are like a radio without an antenna, unable to discern what gifts and talents our souls possess. Unfortunately, most of the people who come to see me are in this state. They have lost touch with their inner guide, and feel uncertain as to who they are and where they are going.

So, as you can see, becoming psychic does not just mean being able to tap into future and past events, or reading the mind of a person you are attracted to at a party. On the most basic level, becoming psychic means learning how to survive. Without our instincts intact, this is a very difficult world. We need our animal senses, our eagle vision, our rabbit hearing, our lizard stillness. The labyrinth is filled with predators. A psychic is light on his feet, careful without being afraid, able to make moves at exactly the right time, seizing opportunities that make his soul flourish. When we are centered and alert, we can avoid much hardship.

When you begin to awaken your psychic powers, many parts of your character that have been repressed will pop to the surface. You will realize that you are many people in one, and that each person in you is there to help you fulfill your destiny. You will learn what role each character is meant to play in your life, how to get your demons to defend your borders rather than sabotage your dreams.

Since I have been giving readings to people, I have become more expressive than ever before. I allow life to speak through me in all its colors. I am now aware that everything works in pairs, that for every light there is also a shadow, and that in order for balance to be achieved, the entire content of our psyche must be embraced.

The more we grow in ourselves, the more we can be there for others. Perhaps you will never have the desire to give formal readings as I have, but even so, once you uncover these deeper instincts, it will affect the people in your life whether you intend it to or not. Even your silence will begin to leave an impression on those around you. A psychic is in harmony with his higher will. Everyone in his presence is influenced to be more in harmony with theirs. In astrology, this is called Saturn energy. Saturn is the god that pushes back onto your path. The farther you are from your authentic self, the harder the push. A psychic has a Saturnian influence on whoever crosses his life. The moment you activate these gifts, you become a teacher.

As you read this book, remember, the access points to the psychic mind are endless. Anything that feeds your soul will enhance these abilities. You might come up with your own way of accessing psychic power that I never mention, something eccentric and whimsical that others may laugh at and not understand. Whenever something like this comes to you, some personal technique that matches your own idiosyncrasies, you must follow it. This is what we are all searching for. The knowledge we get from others is like a rental car, a craft to take us from one point to another in the short term. But our personal truths, concepts that arise from the belly of our soul, are ours to own.

The Holy Child

I don't develop. I am.
—Picasso

 We all come into this world with a deep sense of knowing. We arrive on the planet like the Buddha, fully awake. Our senses are still connected to our spirit; we can see everywhere, hear everything, with no intellectual boundaries to restrict our minds. If we could speak during our first year of life, we would be able to reveal all the secrets of where we came from. If newborns could talk, the mystery of being human would vanish.

As babies, we were clear receptors of psychic information. The instinctual antennae wired in our bodies received pure signals. We were able to interpret exactly what was going on around us, in many dimensions at once. We could sense who was a trustworthy person, what room in the house was conducive to healing, what music nourished our soul.

As infants, we felt the pulse of our life's purpose. It hummed through our cells. We had no fear of expression. When we laughed, even our feet chuckled along wih us. Our anger was complete, a sudden fire that rushed through our bodies and then seconds later was gone. We were like miniature gurus, communicating with the world through silence, through emanations of feeling that transcended words. Without saying a thing, we opened people's hearts, made strangers happy for no reason at all.

Each of us comes into this life for reasons beyond our own personal learning, not only for our soul's growth, but also to help the human species evolve, lift their tired eyes to a new horizon. The blueprint of this journey is stored in our infantile character. In becoming psychically aware, this is the first place we need to look.

Before you go any further, stop reading and take a few minutes of silence to touch this essential part of your being. Close your eyes and breathe deeply. Envision the infant from your past standing in your heart, filling you with its knowledge. He or she might have something they want to tell you right away, some message either in words or feelings that your adult mind has been resisting. If they don't have anything to say to you, just concentrate on their presence. Over time the exercise will become more profound, and it will be easier to receive the messages and impressions the infant is sending you.

As I tell my students, by focusing on this pure center you are giving your soul an entry point through which it can pass vital information. As babies, we were transparencies for truth. Doing this exercise will help you reopen this channel.

If you can, perform this meditation five minutes a day for a month. It will help you absorb the other teachings in the book with less resistance. Focusing on our essence helps erode the walls in our psyche which block our soul's voice. The symbol of the holy child exists in many cultures around the world. Each Christmas we honor its purity, its everlasting joy. When we honor the holy child in us, all the doors of heaven open wide.

Find a photo of yourself that was taken in your first year of life. This will make the visualization more real. When you are finished with the meditation, write in a fresh notebook some of the physical and mental impressions you received (a notebook that you can use as your captain's log for the journey of this book). Write down the memories that came up for you, the colors you saw, the sounds you heard.

The first time I did this exercise, I felt in my head a hot blue light that reached itself through my entire body. The light energized me, made me laugh and cry at the same time. Just that morning I had shown a picture of myself as a one-year-old to my spiritual counselor. I felt the same feeling in my body as I had seen in the picture.

For a moment, I experienced an unusual amount of self-confidence, a belief in myself that erased all my doubts and fears. The feeling said, "I know why I am here." When we were babies, this emotion coursed through us all the time. The more we remember it, the more we can follow our true lives.

The Psychic Growing Up

Your children are not your children, they are the sons and daughters of life's longing for itself.

—Kahlil Gibran

 Very few of us were raised in a family where we felt we fit in, with parents who encouraged us to be ourselves and follow our soul's path. Modern society doesn't inspire this kind of instinctual living. It isn't good for the economy. We are taught to pursue success rather than our own vision.

By five years old many of us already had our entire lives mapped out for us—what schools we were going to attend, what musical instruments we were going to learn, what careers we would pursue. At every turn, the psychic was pushed down into the subconscious. When we needed guidance, we were led to authority figures instead of our own soul. Feeling lost became an ordinary state of mind. Most of my clients come to me in this condition, searching, searching, for a road that will take them home, back to the person they really are.

Primitive cultures had a much different focus. From day one, children were encouraged to trust their inner voice, to believe in the mysterious callings that arose in their being. There were elders specially placed in the community to help young people connect with their soul's path. There were formalized rites of passage, vision quests, group rituals.

In a lecture I attended by Malidoma Somé, a modern-day shaman, he told the story of how his grandfather took him aside when he was four years old and shared with him a psychic dream that foreshadowed his future life in America. In his sleep, the old man had witnessed Malidoma being swallowed by a huge bird and taken to a faraway land. It is this dream that gave Malidoma his name, which means "to be a friend with strangers." Even though the story foretold a tragic event—a young boy leaving the village—the grandfather told it anyway. It was his duty to respect the gods, to help Malidoma live the life he was meant to live.

The moment we make a conscious effort to engage our psychic powers, we will begin to remember the vision that brought us into this life, and step out of any conditioning that is inhibiting this path. To do this, we must first make a thorough examination of our childhood to determine how the psychic was shaped by our early life experiences.

The psychic is an elusive character, influenced by such a myriad of environmental conditions that it is difficult to specify what type of upbringing nurtures this part of us the best. Sometimes going through a dark childhood, with cold alienating parents, can cause the psychic to remain present, as a kind of internal companion to help us through the pain. These instincts can also be reinforced by intimate relationships, by a trip we take to a faraway country, or a creative passion that drives us into depths of feeling.

Just as there are many genres of writing—humor, suspense, poetry, romance—there are many genres of psychic expression. The environment in which we are raised often determines which of these powers we keep and which ones we repress. As babies, our knowing was complete; we had access to a full spectrum of psychic talents. During our early years we gradually lose whatever of these instincts are not stimulated by our surroundings. It is much like Darwinian evolution. Whatever feature of our psyche we use gets stronger; whatever aspects we neglect recede into the unconconscious.

I have divided the psychic into four characters or archetypes: the empath, the seer, the warrior, and the shaman. Simply put, the empath is concerned with the heart, intuition, and emotional feeling. The seer revolves around the intellect and clairvoyant vision. The warrior has to do with the body, the animal instincts that are hardwired into our cells and nervous system. And the shaman governs the soul, the metaphysical principles that shape and influence human life.

It is important that we integrate each character, so that we can have the force and insight necessary to fulfill our soul's path. As you read this book, it will become apparent to you which facet of your psychic ability needs the most attention. Ultimately, the psychic cannot be categorized. These four divisions are just a starting point, a model through which you may examine the various powers that dwell inside you. As you read the next chapters, allow yourself to stop occasionally and ponder how these archetypes have been present in your past, and also how they are expressed in your present life. You will notice there are many places where these characters overlap, blend into one another like shades of paint. For this reason, no two people are psychic in the same way. We each have our own voice.

The Seer

Imagination is more important than knowledge.
—ALBERT EINSTEIN

 When you mention the word "seer," the individual most people think of is Nostradamus, the sixteenth-century French monk who forecast many of the crises of the twentieth century: Hiroshima, the atrocities of the Third Reich, the 1991 Gulf War. Seers are renowned for making prophecy, for seeing through the veil of time and predicting what is going to happen in ten, fifty, or a thousand years. In this field, Nostradamus was one of the best.

But the seer has a much broader role in our psyche than that of prediction. The seer is also responsible for the discovery of new consciousness. When we access the seer's intelligence, we are able to reach our mind into the future or past and retrieve ideas that transform society, that bring humankind another step out of the cave and into the light.

In this vein, the Wright Brothers were seers, as were Socrates, Buddha, Edison, Einstein. Joan of Arc was a seer. (She was also in strong alliance with the warrior.) She followed her internal voices from her parents' farm all the way to Orleans to help the Dauphin become a king and take France back from the English. She was only seventeen when she did this, and living in an era when women were treated as inferior beings. She didn't even know how to read.

You can use the seer's intelligence in any profession. The seer swipes ideas out of the air, advanced perceptions that enhance the performance of any task. In business, people use the seer all the time to forecast economic trends, experiment with new product lines, make intelligent investments. The expression of the seer is also valuable in medical and ecological realms, to help find cures, save forests, develop environmentally safe technologies.

The seer is not just a holy person, but also a realist. Using a fine balance of spiritual insight and common sense, the seer makes predictions that take into account the laws of probability and change. Nature is laden with patterns. The seer is in tune with these patterns and uses them to guide her visions.

At a memorial service for Allen Ginsberg, the seminal beatnik writer, journal entries were read from when he was a ten-year-old boy. The young Allen described himself as a genius, someone who would have a lasting impact on the world. He knew then that after his death, academics would be curious about who he was as a child, and the journal would be there to answer some of their questions. Before puberty, the seer in him already sensed the breadth of his soul's path, and was preparing a catalogue of secrets for all who were interested.

As children, few of us were instinctually drawn to writing the way Ginsberg was; and the seer disappeared into the subconscious without ever being recorded in words. Many of us were taught that our creativity was nothing more than play, and by the time we were adults, respect for our visionary instincts had vanished. The inventions that came to us, the spontaneous ideas, the cures, the political solutions; unless we studied in a field that supported our discoveries, we discarded them as idealistic fancy, and sank another foot deeper into unfulfilling lives.

To stay active, the seer requires outlets, creative channels that push our visionary senses into expression. In childhood the seer is kept awake by enjoyment of the imagination, by daydreaming, visualization, and art. Every time a youngster fingerpaints or builds a house out of wood blocks, she is harnessing the seer, letting her own vision take shape in the world.

Children need to be taught from a young age that the whole universe is at their disposal, that they have sensors in their mind that can pick up information from any dimension, and then express it in their daily life. When children are given this awareness at a young age, as they are in certain Tibetan and Indian cultures, the path to learning is less intimidating, and the mind of the child is more free to inherit the soul knowledge they have earned in past lives.

In my family, the seer was given constant stimulation. My mother read poetry and stories to me from the time I was an infant. There was always music playing in the house, especially baroque music, which is proven by scientists to heal our bodies and open our minds to think without linear constraint. When I spoke philosophically, my parents listened to me as if I had something valuable to offer. They taught me that human intelligence is limitless, that even a child can express ideas that have impact, vision, and meaning.

Unlike the empath and the warrior, the seer rarely becomes overdeveloped, especially in today's society. In the lives of people such as Nostradamus and Jesus Christ, there were moments of visionary overload, where they were driven mad by what they perceived, but such intense visionary states are very uncommon. As a friend of mine once said, the Red Sea is no longer being split apart by a man in a white robe, it is being polluted by oil tankers instead.

With modern education (much of which extinguishes our intuition) and countless hours of television, our visionary senses are usually quite dull by the time we are in our teens. As adults, a lot of us don't even remember our dreams. The seer's eyes are sewn shut, and all we catch are the signals offered to us from the outside, from billboards and magazines rather than from our own imagination.

If we want the planet to thrive in the years to come, we will need to develop ways to keep the seer alive in young people. The seer knows what to do, helps us contact the best possible future and bring some of it back into the present to help humankind evolve. Reviving our psychic abilities is much more valuable than we think. The seer carries a vision of love. Even his wackiest, most far-out ideas, when applied, have a positive effect on the heart.

◎ Seer Exercise

There are many exercises in Part II that will revive your seer abilities. In this chapter, I want to focus on the seer in childhood, getting reacquainted with how these instincts arose in you naturally when you were young. As you read the book, you will realize that you have your own unique style of seeing, one that is as intimate and personal to you as your own breath. Trust it. It will serve you well.

Step one. To begin this exercise, write up a list of all the dreams and visions you had of your adult life before you got there. Everything from the far-out and wild—the astronaut mechanic with twenty children who lived in an ice cream spaceship—to the subtler visions that reveal the private interests of your heart. When you get stuck, go into meditation. When we were young, our visionary senses were constantly probing the future. Getting in touch with these old visions will help you remember key elements of your soul's path. You might have to flesh out the reality from the fantasy, but the gold is still there. If you can't remember them all in one sitting, leave some space open and come back to it.

Step two. Write down any and all predictions, prophecies, inventions, political solutions, and ways to change the world you have had, and put a check mark beside the ones that came true or that you tried to make into a reality. For this part of the excercise, trace your entire past, up until today, right now. This could be a long list. We have all had many visionary moments, in which we saw the future, had a dream that came true, thought of an invention, a philosophy, a song that could help humankind. Again, use meditation to inspire you. You might want to make three columns—one for predictions, one for visionary ideas, and one for prophecies. Prophecies usually have to do with global changes, and predictions are more in line with the self, with family and close friends.

There are a lot of jewels we find along the way that we never take the time to polish. By writing all this stuff down, you will get a clearer picture of all the visionary information that has passed through your psyche, some of which may still be part of your soul's path. Even if you track only small memories, like guessing the color of a sweater your mother got you for Christmas five years ago, or creating an intriguing salad dressing, write them down. It is important to validate every visionary moment. The more we uncover, the more the seer will speak through us.

Step three. List all the creative phases you went through growing up: painting, singing, sculpting, dancing, writing. Place a line under the ones you still wish to pursue. Remember—art is vast; it encompasses many diverse fields, from trumpet playing to origami. Don't judge what is or isn't significant. Put everything you remember down on paper.

The main purpose of this exercise is to recall all the miraculous moments when the seer touched your eyes and made you see. The more deeply you sink into your past, the more of this character you will find. You might remember the time you were painting and stumbled upon an inventive cartoon character, or the time you were sitting in your tree house and had a flash view of your future home. Examine everything you dig up with a careful eye. Come back to it a week or month later to see what moves you. Listen with your intuition to what each memory means. Everything you found, you found for a reason.

Remember, the seer is not limited to precognition. When this character is present in our bodies, we can open up to many different levels of intelligence. Depending on what we require in the moment, the seer will offer it to us: humor, eloquence, mathematical proficiency.

When I did this exercise, to my surprise, I came upon the memory of a time I played a theater game in seventh grade and was taken over by this hilarious voice that made everyone in the class convulse with laughter. The voice belonged to a middle-aged British woman who used words and expressions I had never heard before. Her stories broiled with sarcasm. I could feel her in my body like a separate person, channeling through me with grace and ease.

As I explored the memory, I became aware of a deep desire I have to perform. I had totally forgotten how much passion I have for the stage. My ego had repressed the memory because for some reason it is threatened by the freedom this art form gives me. When I was playing the theater game, I was completely uncensored, able to move in any direction I wanted. I was no longer the diplomat. I could just tell it like it is.

Another memory that resurfaced was the time I foresaw my wife's nationality when I was eleven years old. Under my bed, I kept a copy of an atlas I had received as a birthday present from my parents. The atlas was like a plane ticket for my imagination. It took me all the places I wanted to go without having to leave my room. I was especially interested in the marshlands of the southern United States. I was living in Canada at the time and the snake hunting wasn't very good.

I can't remember exactly how it happened, but during one of

my atlas travels I received the feeling that my future wife was going to come from France, that when I was old enough, I would cross the Atlantic to meet my bride. Twelve years later I met Raïna. She was born in Paris and had a face much like the one I had seen in my daydreams growing up. We got married after knowing each other for only six months. The courting and marriage was like one big *déjà vu*.

The seer might have appeared in your childhood with vivid hair-raising messages, or in ways that are subtle and ordinary. The seer is the messenger that leads us to our career, our position in the world, our future mate, so however discreet the visions were, we need to find them. They hold the key to the real life that our soul wants us to live.

As James Hillman discusses in his book *The Soul's Code,* a lot of the gifts and talents we possess show up in early childhood and adolescence. He calls it the "acorn theory." Inside the acorn, he says, one finds the image of the oak tree that it is destined to become. The seer helps us uncover this blueprint. He is our archaeological supervisor, assisting us in recovering lost treasures that will give us back more of our real self. All we have to do is make a conscious effort to investigate. When we do this, the seer in us responds to the call.

After writing out all that you can remember, take a highlighter and put a stripe on any memory that you think holds the key to some future path. Don't be skeptical. You might be here to do something outrageous, to make computers from nylon stockings or raise cancer healing molecules from organic apple seeds. Breathe. Laugh. The seer is wild. When you look at the faces of those who followed visions, who went out to the edge to bring back information to help the planet grow, you will notice they are unusual, daring, even strange. We must embrace this radical part of us, so that it may find stable residence in our everyday lives.

Last step. Find a picture or symbol of the seer, something to help awaken the awesome visionary being who lives inside you. Place the picture or symbol in a sacred place in your home, an altar of some kind that you can use for this book. It could be as simple as a table with some flowers on it, or a windowsill in your bedroom. The altar will act as a reminder of the journey that you are on, the slow and exciting process of revealing your soul's path.

Here are some people and images that I think fit this category, but let yourself be a judge of who or what is a seer.

> e.e. cummings
> Anaïs Nin
> The North Star
> Shakespeare
> A raven
> Clouds
> Nicola Tesla
> Robert Bly
> Tibetan mandalas

The Empath

It is only with the heart that one can see rightly; what is
essential is invisible to the eye.
—ANTOINE DE SAINT-EXUPÉRY

 The empath enables us to feel other people's experiences in our own body, everything from subtle emotions all the way to physical illness. Teachers,
psychologists, and healers all use the empath to conduct their work. Nature endows us with this gift so that we can
feel our loved ones when they are hurting, either in the same room
or across the globe. Mothers are natural empaths. I heard a doctor
on a radio program say that even when a mother is apart from her
baby, the baby's hunger can sometimes start the flow of breast
milk. She could be ten miles away, and her body will still react.

The empath draws on the intelligence of the heart, teaches us
compassion and the interconnectedness among all living things.
Whenever I think of the empath, an image comes to mind from a
sonnet by the German poet Rilke. In the poem a young man is
being assaulted by a town mob with spears of fire, but miraculously
goes unburned. As the flames near his face, they turn into white
blossoms, because he is standing only in love. When expressed
consciously, the empath has this type of radiance, able to transmute
suffering into joy, to penetrate the severest darkness and expose
the light.

Every time you respond to an intuitive impulse to reach out and care for someone, you are invoking the empath into your life. The empath is reinforced by a childhood in which a person is taught to be considerate of others, an environment where it is safe to talk about feelings and dreams, and there is a physical warmth among members of the family.

The empath becomes overexpressed when a child is pushed into the role of caretaker with one or both of his parents, and is not allowed to develop his or her own identity. When this happens, it is easy to become a slave to other people's needs, to abandon your own passions for the sake of humanity.

In order for the empath to serve us, we must cultivate a healthy sense of self. We must learn how to take care of ourselves before we go outside and try to heal the world. When you have weak boundaries, and a strong empathic character, you become a psychic sponge for all the negativity in your environment, and lose yourself in close relationships.

A student in one of my workshops told me the story of how she was sitting in a science class and suddenly felt a thrusting pain in her cervix. The pain was so bad that she thought she was dying. It turned out that the lady beside her had ovarian cancer, and the empath in her had picked it up.

This is an extreme case of how the empath functions. Most of us will never encounter this instinct in such an intense measure. But if we had a childhood in which we were made to feel responsible for our parents' well-being, or were physically abused, then it is likely that our empathic forces operate in an exaggerated fashion, and we will have to work to balance them out.

If your childhood carried these patterns, and you have a habit of taking on other people's emotions, you can give the empath equilibrium by invoking the warrior. (See the next chapter.) The warrior protects this part of us, provides a shield of light to guard our empathic sensors. Any of us who have been abused need to develop a strong inner warrior. The empath and the warrior are polar opposites. The intensity of the warrior is tempered by the softness of the empath, and in turn, the empath is given protection by the warrior.

Aside from accessing the warrior, there is also a ritual you can do to give the empath strong boundaries. Before meditating, draw an imaginary circle around yourself which defines your space in the world. Then while breathing, imagine the circle growing into an orb of impenetrable light, covering your entire body. Doing this ritual a few minutes a day—prior to meditation or even when you are at work or out with friends—will help you build a healthy aura to filter out negative psychic energy.

Most people aren't aware of how much heavy emotion the empath in them picks up every day. This ritual is like waterproofing your shoes. If you do it consistently, you can walk through the darkest puddles and not get any stains.

◎ Empath Exercise

The empath cannot act in a healthy manner until we release ourselves from the grip of restricting family relationships. I have observed in my readings that in most people the empath is still living in the past, working overtime for other people, when it should be turned inward to heal and guide the self.

Sit quietly somewhere and hold your hand on your heart, feeling your pulse, for two or three minutes. When you are relaxed, visualize yourself as a child between the ages of five and ten, sitting in one of the rooms of the house where you grew up. As if you were holding an interview, call your parents one by one into the room with you. Examine the different sensations in your body with each one of them. Evaluate whether either of them was attached to your empathic senses in a controlling way, and made you feel responsible for their happiness. If this is true for either one, tell them in your mind that you wish to be free of their influence, that you are ready to walk forward as an independent human being.

There might be a number of other people to invite into the room. In order to do this exercise properly, you need to call up all the people who manipulated your heart when you were a child. This might take you into some shadowy areas, but the freedom you'll receive in return is worth it.

In the next stage of the meditation, you need to determine who in your childhood gave you the most space to be yourself, to express all your feelings and private desires without shame. Go through the interview again and see who comes up. This time include your siblings and close childhood friends. When you have found the person, focus your attention on the warmth between you. Recognize this as a healthy expression of the empath, this charge of intimacy in which you are able to remain connected to yourself, and at the same time, physically aware of another person's emotional needs.

Stay in this loving frequency for as long as you want. When you are finished, write some notes in your journal about how you felt connecting with the empath, what images and colors came to mind, and what relationships from your childhood you think still need healing.

For my friend Richard, a memory came up of an old bully who had terrorized him for most of his early life. The bully was so programmed into his subconscious that every time he tried to figure out what he was meant to do in his life, his inner voice was mute. The trauma from the bully blocked the empath from speaking. He couldn't hear what his heart wanted, and thus could not embark on his soul's path.

In my workshops, I tell my students to go back into this meditation at least three or four times to face the people who affected them the most. The meditation becomes like a courtroom. You can yell, scream, curse, swear . . . tell the person all the bad events that happened to you from being enslaved by their drama. The less burdened you are by these old relationships, the more clearly the empath will speak to you and guide you toward your dreams. You can also write letters to these people and burn them. Do whatever you want.

The most psychic thing you can do at any given moment is to give love where it is needed, either to yourself or another person. When the empath is healed, you will find love pouring out of you all the time, a new love, which doesn't involve any loss of self.

You will start to get a feeling of who needs a phone call from you to lift their spirits, what books you should read to open your heart, which doctor is the most caring, who is a trustworthy person, how available someone is for an intimate relationship. The empath will also inform you when you need to slow down and take a rest, a retreat, a breath. The empath is the humanitarian part of us that wants to serve life and contribute some healing to the planet. If we listen, the empath will show us our own specific way.

One final suggestion. Go out and find a statue or picture that is symbolic of the empath that dwells inside you. It could be a tree, a Buddha, or a picture of the sun . . . whatever you like. As with the seer, place the statue in a sacred place in your home, an altar of some kind that you can use for this book. Each time you uncover a new aspect in yourself, it is important to give it a physical representation. The symbol of the empath will remind you to stay open to the voices of your heart, to love yourself and the world around you, and to trust, above all, that you yourself are your own best guide.

The Warrior

It is not by accident that the pristine wilderness of our planet disappears as the understanding of our own inner wild nature fades.

— CLARISSA PINKOLA ESTÉS

 The warrior represents the animal instincts that are hardwired into our brain and nervous system. When people talk about feeling from the gut, or going on impulse, they are talking about the warrior. A warrior doesn't analyze; he takes action, moving with the speed of his awareness in whatever direction his soul wishes him to travel.

The warrior helps you read people, sniffing out the danger zones of any situation. Similar to empaths, warriors gather information through sensors in the body, but it doesn't weaken them. They have healthy boundaries. The energy they pick up passes over them like the wind. Even in the face of danger they remain vital, alive, and dynamic.

Bruce Lee was a warrior. Through his martial arts training he developed eyes all over his skin. He could sense the space around him with the fidelity of cat, and could take on ten attackers blindfolded. Martin Luther King had warrior energy. His speeches made people feel inspired from their feet all the way to their brain. The warrior connects us to the earth, to the body, to the subtle pulses of nature that keep us feeling healthy and full of life.

In his best-selling book *Emotional Intelligence*, Daniel Goleman explains how much of the violence we experience in our culture is due to the fact that our brains have not caught up with our modern style of living. The impulse to chase animals, stalk through the forest, and fight opposing tribes still moves though our bodies. When we don't have a release for these energies, they spring out of us unconsciously, and harm us rather than support our growth.

People who are raised on a farm, or around tough parents, are prone to develop the warrior, as a response to the intensity of their surroundings. My father carried this character in abundance. He was a man of the old world; he liked to hunt, weight-lift, ride horses. He also had a brutal temper, and could go from being a saint to a tyrant in the flash of an eye. Being in his presence taught me how to harness great amounts of energy in my body, and gave me instincts like a marine.

When the warrior part of us is never initiated, the world can feel like a dangerous place. We need the warrior to get through the grind of daily living, to make decisions in the moment without fear. The warrior is the psychic part of us that lives beyond thought, that knows things through instinct rather than analysis. New York City has a lot of warrior energy. Just walking on the streets there brought this part out in me.

As children, our bodies crave a feeling of wildness. When we don't get a chance to experience this, through a sport or some other physical challenge, it is difficult for us to feel confident, to be grounded in the world and act from our own foundation.

On the other hand, going through a war or an abusive upbringing can make the warrior blown out of shape and cruel or, in some cases, meek or nonexistent. When this happens, we have to go the opposite route. We need to find soothing practices, such as meditation and massage therapy, which heal the emotional trauma in our bodies before we turn on the flame. This is a long process, and requires a great deal of physical nurturing before our bodies learn that not everyone is out to get us.

Since we have become city dwellers, many of us have lost connection with the warrior. When this part of us is repressed, we make easy targets for all sorts of invasions, from rape to deadly viruses, and our decision making loses its accuracy and quickness.

It was not that long ago that we were hunting for food and following the light of stars and the moon. We need to have a practice that keeps the warrior active, that keeps us breathing from our bellies, and our animal senses alert to all the sudden opportunities that help us stay on our soul's path. Martial arts, archery, mountain climbing, hiking: any of these will bring the warrior into action, keep us alive and centered in the grind of daily living.

The warrior teaches us how to give love in the body, and at the same time, how to say no and mean it. As the knights of old used to say, you need to become a poet before you are given a sword. With the help of the other psychic characters, the warrior's fire is kept in check.

◎ Warrior Exercise

Go to a place in nature where as a child you felt invigorated and alive: the ocean, under a tree, the mountains, the desert. If this is not possible, go somewhere that reminds you of that place. Plan on spending the afternoon there with your journal, your pen, your imagination, and a lot of invigorating breath.

As I mentioned, the warrior is linked to our animal nature. To begin the exercise, go into your childhood memory and pick out your favorite warrior animal, one that gave you a feeling of strength, wildness, and protection. Sit comfortably in your nature spot, and write a page about this animal, all the qualities that you related to and admired growing up. Write about the animal's eyes, its fur or scales, about how it defends itself, how it shows affection, what sounds it makes, how it walks and hunts for food. Don't just write scientifically. Get into the spirit of the animal, the secrets of its being.

The child in you might have worshipped a particular dinosaur or an imaginary creature that only you knew about. If you want, you can write about one of these instead. It's up to you.

Once you have written a page, close your eyes and meditate on the life force of the animal, the particular energy that animates the creature's movements. Imagine the instincts of the animal pouring into your blood. Adjust your breath to the speed and rhythm of the animal. Does the animal breathe through his mouth or his nose? How does the animal perceive the world? Does it think? If so, how does the thinking feel? What part of the world stands out to the animal the most? Let your body feel the same sensors on your skin that the animal has, the same instinctual receivers.

Stay in this meditation for about ten minutes. Keep expanding your inner world to include the animal, to merge with its rhythm and breath.

In a certain style of kung fu, the students incorporate different animal personalities into their fighting techniques, to enliven their bodies to new speeds and rhythms. As children we did the same thing. We imitated animals to keep our instincts active, our bodies in tune with the plants, trees, and people around us.

Many Native American tribes use animal symbols to honor man's instinctual relationship with nature. As part of their initiation into adulthood, young men and women are sent into the forest to fast and wait for a vision to determine what animal spirit will be their guide. This meditation I have given you draws on these same principles. Remember, the warrior is not about fighting or killing; it is a link to our own sacred fire, the deep primordial forces that influence our lives. Only when we ignore it, and put it in a cage, does it revolt against us and harm others.

When you are done meditating, without thinking, write down a list of all the physical activities you were drawn to as a child that stimulated the warrior in you. List all the sports, hobbies, and games that served this character in your psyche. What you are looking for are activities or situations in which you felt intensely alive and dynamic in your body, such as rock climbing, boxing, tennis. Just recently I have remembered the passions of my own childhood in which the warrior was expressed: archery, martial arts, rope climbing, swimming, hiking, fort building, jogging. In the last two years I have integrated many of these activities back into my life, and they have enhanced my psychic ability and physical alertness to an amazing degree.

Even if you are not able to perform the activities with the same vitality, it is still worth bringing them back into your life. Select a few and begin performing them once or twice a week. This will stimulate the cellular memory in your body in which the warrior was fully active. You will be more awake in your skin. In times of need, your instincts will be close at hand.

As much research has proven, our bodies contain a vast amount of knowledge, and are able to heal themselves with miraculous built-in cures. When we blend into our life suitable instinctual practices, we unlock psychic gifts that the mind alone cannot reveal. Contrary to popular opinion, psychic ability does not just reside in our head. We have sensors all over our body, telephone lines in our every cell. As children we were intuitively drawn to activities that kept this intelligence flowing. It was part of our magic. We knew what to do to keep our psyches fully alive.

After your wonderful afternoon of writing, meditating, and remembering, go out and find a symbol of the warrior, some picture or statue that will remind you of this intelligent fire that lives inside you, and put it next to the symbol of the empath. The journey goes on.

The Shaman

We are departing for the skies.
Who has a mind for sight-seeing?
—RUMI

 We all have a shaman living inside us, a wizard who dwells at the crossroads where our spirit and flesh meet. When we make love, meditate, pray, dance, compose music, this ancient part of us awakens, animates our bodies, and takes us traveling into the dreamworld from which we came.

It is the shaman in us that can feel the presence of dead relatives, communicate with spirits, give a healing to a friend in another city, merge with the sound of a wave, a bird cry, or a violin. The shaman has one foot planted on the earth and the other stretched into eternity. Every time we fall asleep, we brush by the doorway of the shaman, that elusive realm of thoughts and images that stay hidden during most of our waking lives.

Shamans communicate through symbols and energy patterns. They are able to read the inner language of plants and animals; they activate natural forces with breath and spoken word. In many aboriginal cultures, the shaman is the healer and guide of the community, knowledgeable in herbal medicine, meteorology, astronomy, childbirth, death. They dress in eccentric costumes, in bird feathers and animal bones, and conduct group trances that help the tribe strip their human masks and merge with the gods.

In modern times, the shaman is still present, but we experience his world mostly as a spectator. Many of us don't have a tolerance for real-life magic. We can deal with it on the screen—see an alien morph into a swamp monster, or watch John Travolta shoot light from his fingertips—but when the mystical appears in our own life, when our lover's face turns into a sage, or we hear an old voice rise up from our unconscious, we feel that we are going mad, and do everything in our power to make the mystery go away.

The shaman is the part of us that can tolerate chaos and break-down, that is able to roam beyond the borders of sanity to gather energy and harness it in the world. The cliché image of the mad scientist is a pretty accurate portrayal of the shaman at work. When we have a healthy empath and warrior to support us, we can make our descent into our private laboratory, drink our secret potion, and arrive back into life more healthy and sound than when we left.

We all need to go crazy now and then, to dance outside the circle and spread our uncivilized wings. The human desire to space travel, visit mystical dimensions, write poetry, or watch fireworks, are all cravings of the shaman. When we feed these cravings in a healthy manner, rather than with drugs and alcohol, we can move onto our soul's path with greater fluidity, building pyramids, com-posing music, or accomplishing tasks that defy earthly principles.

The comedian Dennis Miller, in his book *Rants,* jokes about this part of us that longs to dissolve into light.

". . . you're never going to stop the human need for release through altered consciousness. The government could take away all the drugs in the world and people would spin around on their lawns until they fell down and saw God."

Many Westerners who do call forth the shaman do so with an air of escapism, trying to eliminate human pain once and for all and live happily in the stars. In studying the lives of such artists as Van Gogh, Jim Morrison, Jack Kerouac, you can feel that their mystical explorations were motivated by a lot of unresolved emo-tional pain, propelling them into other worlds at an almost suicidal speed.

As we step into the shaman's shoes, we need also to heal and resolve our past. Marion Woodman, a renowned Jungian analyst, refers to this in many of her books. She believes that if we engage our spirit powers without repairing the psychological trauma stored in our bodies, then the forces we harness will only cause us more pain. It would be like buying a more powerful engine for your car before fixing your alignment. You are asking for trouble.

By the same token, we can't ignore our shamanistic urges either. When these instincts are repressed, they can control us from behind the scenes, draw us into spells of delusion, paranoia, depression, or anxiety. As Miller said, humans need a spiritual release. Without the shaman, we lose our overview, feel trapped in a meaningless world, with no breathing apparatus to reach the sky.

As children, most of us were not given any assistance to develop the shaman. Rather than deepening our psychic powers, we learned to rely on food, cigarettes, drugs, and material possessions to replace the real magic the shaman part of us seeks. If you notice, as the years go by, toys keep getting more and more fancy, and children's eyes, more and more dull. The shaman is being crushed by technology, put into a bright box along with many of our other natural psychic instincts.

In order for the shaman to survive into adulthood, a child's fantasy life must be given credibility. The old story about children having imaginary friends who are actually spiritual guides, and losing contact with these beings because their parents ridicule them, is a common example of how a mother or father can destroy a child's link with the "other side." For the shaman to grow, there must be a tone of sacredness in the home, a belief in invisible forces, daily rituals such as prayer and meditation, which bring the family together to honor and experience the mysteries of life.

I am fortunate that my parents provided a rich context for the shaman to develop. My father had a passion for astronomy and Native American culture, and my mother, who is an internationally renowned psychic, introduced me to the psychic arts: tarot cards, deep trance healings, astrology, automatic writing. She and I both made a departure from Catholicism at the same time, a year after my father's death, and immediately dove into our own metaphysical practices which dramatically expanded our lives.

Since then my spirituality has evolved, becoming synthesized with different fields of psychology and art. From years of study, I have discovered that the shaman doesn't always have to be sought out through serious methods and solemn rituals. Creative play can engage this part of us just as easily, and often in a more authentic manner. When the shaman is called forth spontaneously, through role-playing and sacred games, we may slip into the other world with less pretense and more wonder. When we let ourselves have fun with the shaman, superstition dissolves, and we can explore the depths of our soul with delight rather than fear.

The shaman also comes to life in moments of true intimacy. When two people are naked with each other, exposing their secrets and hidden dreams, an atmosphere is created in which the shaman can speak and reveal details of past lives, karmic patterns, or startling perceptions which illuminate our soul's path. As Jesus Christ said, "When two or more come together, I am there." The shaman is inspired by soulful company, by the trusting bond of friendship, marriage, and family.

Living in California, I have noticed that the shaman is coming out of hiding more and more. There are many sacred theater classes, vision quests, sweat lodges, and meditation seminars, where people are given a safe context to break down their walls and express their souls. Much of it is still experimental, an imitation of old tribal practices, but at least we are searching, reaching down into our bodies to touch this ancient being that dreams our life. The shaman is there to give us guidance during changing times, to keep us connected to the universal mind.

⊚ Shaman Exercise

Step one. To begin this exercise, make a list of the most intense mystical experiences from your childhood up to yesterday, times when reality expanded and you caught a glimpse of the eternal. You might have seen an angel, heard the voice of a dead relative, seen a bright light around your mother's face . . . or the experience might have been more personal, something unique only you can describe. There is a misconception that the spirit world appears the same way to all of us. This is not true. For one person, angels might have wings and halos, and for another person, they might look like giant red stars. What is mystical for you might be ordinary to someone else, and vice versa. Be your own judge of what fits this category. Meditate for a few minutes and write down every memory you can find. Elaborate. Write about how your body felt, what you did after the experience, how long it stayed with you.

The spirit world is most vivid when we are at a crossroads, stepping beyond our comfort zone into a more passionate mode of living, or during a crisis, such as a car accident or robbery, when our life is being threatened. In these situations the shaman jolts us to attention, activates our adrenaline, gives us the speed and power we need to escape the danger. Any situation where you were standing at the edge, where the realization of life and death pulsed through you, is worth studying. There might have been a presence there you didn't see, some guardian that was leading you to safety. Sniff around. Use your internal vision to examine the whole scene.

You can also call forth into your memory times when you were lost and miraculously found your way home. At these moments, we are always being directed by spiritual forces, taken care of whether we realize it or not.

If you find a memory that you really like, some jewel of the past, just sit with it and let it fill you up. You couldn't have a more foolproof method of awakening your psychic powers. Memories such as these are like personalized teachings. They rewire your antennae, reminding you of what it feels like to be in harmony with your soul's path.

Step two. Examine your early years and see if you can find any rituals you did growing up that made you feel in tune with the universe. We all did something. The instinct to pray and worship is wired into all of us. I'll share a secret with you. When I was twelve, I had a ninja temple in one of the downstairs rooms of my house. After my brother and sister moved out, I plastered about thirty holy pictures on the wall, put some velvet curtains on the carpet to kneel on, hung my bamboo swords on the cabinet, and presto, I had a ninja temple. Whenever I felt sad or alone, I would go down there and meditate. It was my private church. I built it all on my own.

When we were children, we all had our own way of honoring life. When we integrate these practices into our adult character, suddenly we have a gateway, a natural mode of worship where our soul can meet with us. Again, let yourself be the judge of what is a sacred ritual. When you explore your childhood, you might decide that fishing was how you connected with god, or reading books, or building paper kites. If you can, invite some of these activities back into your life. Even if the activity is just something small, it will give you a feeling of wholeness, an opening for the shaman to come through and share his magic.

In addition to my ninja temple, trees were another window to the other world. When I wasn't climbing them, I was sitting with my father and staring at the large poplars that lined our driveway. They awakened me. It was the same with old men. I have many memories of talking with old men, at bus stops, nursing homes, in the park, being swept away by their slow wisdom, their carefully spoken tales. Old men popping up from nowhere, making the shaman in me smile and laugh.

After you are finished with this exercise, go out and find a symbol or picture of the shaman as you have for the other characters. This should be very easy. In almost every New Age shop you walk into nowadays there are Buddha statues, Native American carvings, crystals, stones, mandalas. Get something that will help you invoke the shaman into your life, something that speaks specially to you.

In the chapters to come, I will give you many exercises to awaken the shaman. You will learn how to interpet symbols, how to connect with spirit guides, how to create personal rituals. Remember, the shaman goes beyond mere prediction. When we are in touch with these instincts, we become an architect, in league with the forces of the universe that promote change and healing in the world. We learn how to set ourselves and others free from the bondage of the past and travel into our real lives.

PART II

Activating
the Seer

The Eye That Sees

I have always been able to see what others were unable to
see; and what they did see, I did not see.
                                        —SALVADOR DALI

 When I was a kid, one of my greatest fears was to go
blind, to lose my ability to see. Somehow I always
knew how precious it was to have eyes, to be able to
absorb the light and color of the outside world into
my body. There is so much we can learn by just watching a leaf
fall, a child tie his shoe, a pigeon chase after a piece of bread. The
old haiku poets of Japan knew this well. The basis of their art was
simply to observe life, to be so totally present and clear in the mind
that a ripple of moonlit water could push them into enlightenment.

Nowadays, the only time most of us feel visually satisfied is
when we are sitting in a dark theater with popcorn on our lap.
We crave car chases, explosions, gunfire, sharp obnoxious images
hurled into our brain. A tree is not enough. We want an angel to
come ripping through the air, a blaze of light to knock us off our
feet.

In order to develop your seer abilities, you need to refine your
senses like the haiku poets of Japan. I always tell my students to
spend fewer hours in front of the television and more time in
nature, attuning their vision to what is real, to the subtle beauty
of flowers, trees, and running water. In nature, the eye can travel

deeply, exploring delicate levels of being. On a television program, the images are pre-made. There are no hidden dimensions. When you stare at William Shatner, he remains William Shatner. The doorways of perception are locked.

Sometimes during a reading a client will ask me if I am gathering information on them by how they look, by the clothes they are wearing and the jewelry around their neck, as opposed to receiving impressions in my mind. They think that being psychic means visions that come from thin air, and that if I am reading them based on their appearance, that I am cheating.

My answer is that I read everything, from hair color all the way to past lives. Like a painter, I employ a wide range of sight. The way someone lights their cigarette is as important to me as the images that float through my head.

When you really open your eyes, everything tells you a story. You can sense how someone was raised by the way they smile, how relaxed they are by the way they hold their hands when they're talking.

Psychics in China know this very well; they do readings on the whole body—the feet, the mouth, the forehead. It is not cheating to be observant. Whether you gain your insights from a person's eyes or a set of Tarot cards doesn't matter. When your senses are in tune with your soul, you could read a person's napkin and give them insight into their life. Gypsies read tea leaves and coffee grains. The seer can find meaning in anything.

In the Western world, we have gotten hooked on the idea of inner and outer, back and front, deep and shallow. When you close your eyes, it is fantasy; when you open them, it is reality. In Zen Buddhism, the same distinctions are not made. The inner and outer worlds are one. The dream you have at night is just as real as the dream you have during the day. However deeply you can look at a tree, you can look at yourself.

The only difference between a psychic vision and ordinary seeing is the depth to which you are looking. Just as you can aim a telescope at your neighbor's window or the moon in the sky, you can train your eyes to perceive many levels of existence, from the aura around your cat, to the bright zones of the afterlife.

When I teach people seeing, I try not to tell students what is sacred and what isn't. Someone might be naturally inclined to see the soul through mathematical shapes; another person might perceive mythological characters or magnetic fields. For me to come along and tell a student what they should see would be arrogant and misleading. Could you imagine someone telling Monet not to put so much purple on his water lilies, or suggesting to Rembrandt that his nudes are too pale?

Unfortunately, this is how many of us are taught the psychic arts. We are told that the spirit world looks a certain way, and that unless we see it in that form, we are not having an authentic visionary experience. The truth is, no two people see the same universe. Deepak Chopra's model of the quantum field is just as subjective as a Keith Haring painting, or a Paleolithic cave drawing. The imagery our soul projects into our minds is different for each of us. It is influenced by our age, our culture, our sex, our beliefs. At ten, we might have a vision of God with a beard and scepter; at forty, we might see Elvis; and at seventy, it might just be our grandchild's face.

For an artist, whatever he is looking at has meaning. He doesn't need to use the word "clairvoyant," because the whole universe is holy. Whether it be a spirit that appears out of thin air, or a piece of fruit on the table, it all has soul.

Each human breakthrough begins from a new depth of seeing. With the invention of the telescope, Galileo showed us that the earth was not the center of the solar system, which gave early Catholics a much-needed head spin. In the nineteenth century, van Leeuwenhoek discovered that matter was not solid, that it was made of small building blocks called cells. With this knowledge, doctors could stop their bloodletting, and get to work on some much-needed cures.

When a person uncovers a new vision of reality, and shares it with the world, it travels like wildfire, enhancing everything it touches: films, computers, machines, relationships. In the fascinating book *We've Had a Hundred Years of Psychotherapy and the World's Getting Worse*, Michael Ventura talks about how quickly visionary themes are able to spread through culture, how early-twentieth-century painting styles such as cubism and surrealism zipped from brain to brain like a psychic virus until a whole society began to see in a new way.

A thousand years from now, who knows how we'll see things? Scientists may discover that atoms and quarks are not the essential reality. They may find out that everything is red, that behind the atomic curtain, there is nothing but deep, passionate, alluring red.

If morphing is already old hat, anything is possible that far down the road.

◎ Seeing Exercise

This exercise will prepare you for the next chapters, in which you will learn how to expand your vision to see into other times and places. It is a wake-up exercise, like a cup of coffee for the eyes. Enjoy yourself. Don't feel that you have to rush through the book. Go at your own speed.

Step one. Go to a bookstore or a library and visit the art section, where they have those huge glossy books filled with paintings. You can make it a field trip with a lover or a friend. Give yourself time. Pretend you are living in the Renaissance, before the invention of *People* magazine, when art mattered. Go through the books as if you have never seen any of the painters before, and be especially open to painters whose work you have never seen before. If you have not been in the painting world for a while and feel the need for a starting point, try one of these artists: Salvador Dali, Alex Grey (especially his book *Soul Mirrors),* Georgia O'Keeffe, or Claude Monet.

The books you are drawn to will contain images and colors that resonate with your soul. Go through the pages at a leisurely speed. When you find a painting that really moves you, that stirs your optic cells, sit there and stare at it for a while. Let the light and color fill you up.

If you live in a big city, you could visit a museum instead. Anaïs Nin, the famous American diarist, said that when she was living in New York and needed a taste of heaven, she would visit a small museum and sit for an hour in front of an eight-foot painting of the sun. The painting was her god. Just looking at it made her feel healed and refreshed. Few of us give ourselves beauty when we need it. Anaïs Nin was one of those rare people who knew what to do to keep her soul alive. She thought that artists were the true priests, that in a dark time, it was not religious teachers, but rather poets, painters, and sculptors, who carried the light.

Step two. Write a paragraph about your favorite painting, why it touched you, what it was about it that awakened your soul. Write stream of consciousness. *I liked the painting because it made me think of god and being a little kid and no end to wonder with yellow warmth and excitement in my belly*. Let your pen go wild. No censorship.

Step three. When you enter back into reality—your home, office, or the coffee shop next door—see if you can perceive in the objects and people around you the same level of beauty you saw in the painting. Rarely do painters create strictly from the unconscious. Most of them combine their hidden selves with the world around them, blending spirit with matter in their own masterful way. See what it feels like to perceive life through this double lens, to bring your soul vision into the mundane, to see in the face of a stranger the same wonder and intensity that lived in the painting.

If you have difficulty doing this, close your eyes, visualize the painting, and then open them again, two or three times. Doing this will help you draw the painting outside of you. This is the role of any psychic artist, to bring the beauty that lives inside them into the outer world, to share it like food with fellow human beings.

If the painting you chose was famous, buy yourself a print and put it somewhere in your home. It will act as a reminder of how your soul sees the world, keeping your eyes attuned to beauty as you pass through the day

Seeing Colors

Poles apart, I am the color of dying and you are the color
of being born. Unless we breathe in each other, there
can be no garden.

—RUMI

 The fact that we describe many of our emotional states
with colors is not a coincidence. He was seeing red.
She was green with envy. I'm feeling blue. We say
these things because they are true. As scientists have
confirmed, the human body is surrounded by colorful magnetic
fields, a boundary of light called the aura. When we shift from one
emotion to another, the colors around us change. Viewed through
the third eye, our bodies are not static. We are like a painting that
is always moving, a piece of kaleidoscopic art.

As children, we were more connected to this primary level of
seeing. We spoke our feelings with crayons and fingerpaints. When
we saw an orange balloon, we practically fell out of our strollers
trying to touch it. Not so long ago we'd been floating around
without a body, communicating with other spirits in subtle lan-
guages of color and vibration. That's why the orange excited us.
It was a familiar language. We knew what it meant.

An important step in developing the seer is to bring this color
awareness back into your life. A lot of the messages I receive in
my readings are color-coded. When someone asks a question about
his family or a problem at work, sometimes the first thing I see in

my mind is a color. It flashes into my psyche, leaving a glowing impression all through my cells.

I interpret the color in two ways. First, I feel it. I breathe it into my body, allowing myself to receive all the subtle nuances the color is carrying, its hidden flavors and insights. Then I apply it to my internal color chart. From my studies of the aura and color therapy, I have a basic understanding of what each color means in reference to our spiritual and psychological development. From these two sources, I am able to translate a great deal of information to my client. I am like a fashion designer; I've got the fabric and now I can design my dress.

I have composed a list of the seven main colors of the human body (in accordance with the seven chakras) and how you can use them to stay more true to your soul's path. Each color is like a separate instinct, which can be activated to give you a broader field of awareness.

Following the list of colors, there are two exercises I invented which will teach you how to project and receive colors across time and space. They are simple, yet tremendously effective. They will serve you well.

If, as you are reading, you realize that you have your own interpretation for a color that is different from mine, by all means use it. I am just conveying themes, standard healing properties I have discovered through my work. At all times when reading this book, "To thine own self be true."

⦿ Red

Red is a power color. It has to do with survival, with the primal forces that ground us in our identity. It is the color of the root chakra, the energy center located at the base of the spine. Red gives us strong boundaries in relationships, encourages us to fight for what we believe in, and keeps our feet firmly planted on the earth. If a person exudes a lot of red, it means they are sexual, combative, feisty, willing to go the extra mile to get what they want. When I think of red, I think of Madonna, Henry Rollins, Gary Oldman; they are all artists who use their passion and fierceness to cross lines, to expose the hidden, fiery layers of the soul.

The message I get for many of my women clients is to drench themselves in red: red shirts, red paintings, red sculptures. A lot of women need to be reminded that they can express red feelings, that their wildness is as important as their nurturing.

If you have troubling taking a stand, remaining centered in stressful situations, or facing authority figures, you probably need more red in your life. You can perform meditations on the color, imagine it filling your body like a hot liquid, or you could focus on a red mandala, a red Buddha, or a red flower, and draw the color in from the outside.

Doing anything physically aggressive will also invoke red. Martial arts, African dance, Holotropic breath work: any of these will awaken your blood, turn on your red senses, and give you more dynamic energy to face life.

◎ Orange

Orange is the color of creativity. It has to do with art, procreation, invention, spontaneity. It is the color of the pelvic chakra, the energy center located just above the sex organs. It is no surprise that we drink orange juice in the morning. Orange is a wake-up color; it restores our vital energy. When a client is feeling stuck, heavy with worries, I sometimes advise him to meditate on the color orange. It's the equivalent of going to the circus on your lunch break. When you return, you will be much happier.

For artists and business people, I advise putting something orange in your studio or office. It will help you stay open to impulses, to the flash inspirations that come from the fairies and muses, that gives your work an original flavor.

The same applies if you want to have a baby. You could place some orange flowers next to your bed, to invoke an atmosphere of fertility and new growth. You could also do visualizations in which you imagine your womb filled with orange light, like a small orchard, welcoming your future child.

People like Robin Williams, who thrive on wild, comedic outbursts, usually have a lot of orange in their aura. Orange says stop being serious, put down the newspaper, go play Monopoly with your kids, pull out the Twister board, get on your hands and knees, bark like a dog. If you have trouble lightening up, being playful for no reason at all, orange can help you. Like a tollgate, it will halt the flow of mental traffic, and dissolve your self-image fears, so you can let loose and be a kid again.

◎ Yellow

The color yellow has two main themes, thought and action. When you are in deep concentration reading Shakespeare or building an intricate model, your magnetic field will be charged with yellow. Yellow also appears around you when you are expressing your will, using concentrated force to make something happen, such as closing a deal, climbing a mountain, or getting someone to go out with you.

Yellow is the color of the navel chakra, the energy center located an inch below the solar plexus. The expression "fire in the belly" refers to the hot yellow energy that passes through your stomach when your body is living out the commands of your soul, doing what needs to be done at exactly the right moment in time. Malcolm X probably had a lot of yellow in his aura, as do Robert Bly and Maya Angelou.

If you wish to make a life-altering commitment, such as buying a house, taking a trip to Africa, or starting a new business, but are too afraid to act, yellow is the color you need to focus on. The same goes if you want your mind to be quicker, to be able to handle more tasks, balance your checkbook without a calculator, assimilate quantum physics . . . yellow will assist your development.

To enhance your mental capacities, while you are studying or taking a test, imagine your brain expanding with yellow light, like a large sunflower, reaching outward in all directions, absorbing and recalling information with luminous rays.

To conquer your decision-making fears, you can perform meditations where you visualize in the center of your stomach a ball of yellow fire, spreading from your belly all through your body. This will strengthen your will, help you chop through resistance, and give you the impetus you need to step forward into the unknown.

◎ Green

Green is the color of love and healing. When you are in deep rapport with a friend, communicating with intuition and feeling, your aura is filled with green, like ivy circulating your body. Green is the color of the heart chakra, the energy center located in the middle of the chest. People such as Mother Teresa, John Bradshaw, and Nelson Mandela are bearers of this sacred color; it is in their words, their profound humanitarian achievements.

When a client is feeling alienated and shut off from the world, I advise him to draw green into his life, to surround himself with plants and flowers, to take more walks in nature, go camping, plant a tree. When you absorb green into your body, you can heal old trauma, forgive someone from the past, or create art that moves people to tears.

If you have just met a lover or a new friend, you could do a visualization where you see rays of green light weaving you together. This will inspire a feeling of trust and openness, the safety you need to reveal your private self.

When a mother has a new baby, her being is flooded with green. Green is the color of mending, of two or more things coming together as one. Wherever there is harmony, there is green. Individuals who emanate this color know the importance of diplomacy, tact, moderation, balance. They might be emotional, but it is coming from the right place. Their heart is transmitting its song.

◉ Blue

Blue is the color of release and soulful feeling. A blues singer takes his sorrow, pain, or anger, and throws it into music. There is a wide range of feeling in the color blue, everything from depression to ecstatic peace, from Fats Domino to Enya. Blue is the color that draws us down into what is real, that makes us face what we are hiding from, stare into ourselves until we see the truth.

Blue is the color of the throat chakra, the energy center located behind the larynx. Doing a meditation on blue will promote relaxation, getting you in touch with your inner world, the stable reality that exists underneath a worried mind. Blue is soothing, enclosing, hypnotic, endless.

If you have trouble expressing yourself, you can do a visualization where you imagine your throat opening into a spiral of blue light. Doing this before a speech or a seminar will inspire your words, allow you to improvise and uncover spontaneous ideas that enrich your topic.

People who are in touch with blue are often reflective and introverted. They probe life, sink into it deeply and uncover specific, hidden truths. They are intellectual archaeologists, explorers of the unconscious. Anaïs Nin, Carl Jung, the Buddha; I feel all these people had at their essence a sublime shade of blue.

When you need sanctuary in a crowded room, a boundary of silence, you can imagine yourself surrounded by a field of blue, as if you were lying on your back in a swimming pool. Blue mutes disturbing frequencies, gives you the buoyancy of water, and preserves your individual space.

◉ Violet

Violet is the color of vision and insight. Inventors, psychics, poets, and visionaries all have a high concentration of violet in their aura. Violet is associated with the third-eye chakra, the energy center located in the center of the forehead. When you receive images or pictures from your soul, they are sent to you through violet light. Violet is the Federal Express of colors; it allows you to project and receive ideas without speaking, take knowledge from your soul and integrate it into your life.

Violet also helps you review the past with extreme clarity or, like a probe, reach into the future. It inspires a feeling of timelessness, of objectivity, and broad seeing. If your vision is blocked, and you feel disconnected from your soul's path, focusing on the color violet will give you direction and guidance.

It is beneficial when you are starting a project or company to visualize it in your mind surrounded by violet light, maybe even include a trace of it in your business logo. This will keep you and your colleagues open to higher thinking, inspired ideas, and creative solutions.

A violet flower or figurine in your bedroom will assist you in remembering your dreams; you will have more lucid sleep states, and when you wake up in the morning, you'll remember the stories that passed through your mind.

When you are in the presence of a person or being who has a lot of violet in his aura, your mind will blossom with visionary ideas. You will experience what Rilke called, "An incandescence of the intellect."

◉ White

White is the color of divine understanding. When you have white in your aura, it means you are in contact with a higher intelligence, a mind beyond your own. White is the color of the crown chakra, the energy center at the top of the skull. When this part of us is open, we can experience the presence of angels and guides, and see the God-force in all living things.

White can be used as a protective field, to keep out undesirable elements: television static, radiation, viruses. Many modern conveniences, such as air conditioners and microwaves, weaken our magnetic fields, making us more prone to sickness and disturbed mental states. With the protection of white light, you can enter an artificial atmosphere—a mall or an office—and be less affected, stroll under fluorescent lights for an hour, and come out feeling fine.

If you are a nurse or a doctor, performing a daily exercise where you sit quietly and envision yourself surrounded in white light will keep your immune system strong. It is no coincidence that most medical clothing is white. White repels illness and creates a boundary through which negative forces cannot enter.

It is said that when we die, we enter the afterlife through a spiral of white light. The best way to overcome our fear of death is to familiarize ourselves with this transition while our body is still healthy. Meditation is our best preparation. It opens our crown chakra, allowing us to explore other dimensions before our number is called. We encounter what poets call "the white wings of death," a state of pure freedom. White is the beginning and the end. When I think of white, a line from a Jim Morrison song comes to mind. "Can you picture what we'll be, so limitless and free?" This is the message of white.

◎ Projecting and Receiving Colors

Sit with a partner in a relaxed environment and have him or her think of a primary color: red, blue, or yellow. Close your eyes and try to sense what color it is. For the person who is thinking of the color, visualize it emanating from you like mist, reaching across space and touching your partner's mind. For the person who is receiving the color, let your whole body be an instrument of sight. Allow the color to enter you from your toes all the way to your head.

Say the color out loud twice; once when you begin, and then again after two or three minutes of receiving. We all absorb things at different speeds. Find out how you operate, how long it takes for you to grasp what is being offered. Is your first instinct better? Or does your accuracy improve with time?

Do the exercise twice on each side, and then discuss what happened. When you feel ready, add more colors: green, violet, orange, white. You can also send your partner a color long distance, when she is at work or visiting another city. Tell her when you will be sending the color, and have her call you afterward to inform you what she received. Be inventive. Perform this exercise in as many ways as you want.

Projecting and receiving colors is an ancient mode of healing. Now that you know what the different colors mean, experiment by sending yourself and the people around you emanations of color throughout the day. For example, if you sense someone is lonely, you could envision a ray of green light entering their heart, accompanied by a thought of healing. If you are heading up a business meeting and you wish everyone to be open to your ideas, before you go to the office, you could visualize the boardroom swarming with violet light.

You will be amazed how well this works. When used with love and conviction, colors have great power; they are one of the most practical and effective ways to enhance life.

◎ Reading Your Own Colors

At each stage of our lives we exude one color more than the rest. It is like a base note, a magnetic frequency that draws us into a particular field of learning. Some of us ride a color all the way to the grave, and others change it too quickly, before any real knowledge has been absorbed.

If you can determine what color is wishing to be expressed through you at each phase of your growth, and follow it to its completion, you can make huge evolutionary leaps in a single lifetime. You can achieve what psychologists call "wholeness," a state of mental, physical, and spiritual refinement.

Since we are creatures of comfort and habit, a lot of us get stuck in one color, one expression of the soul, and develop resistance to other shades of being. A lot of men get trapped in the red zone— aggression, competition, power—and never make it into green or blue, the rich expanses of intuition and feeling. A lot of spiritual seekers get trapped in the white and violet realms, and disassociate from the intelligence of their lower half, the animal instincts which motivate us to protect our space, earn a living, laugh, dance, and play.

You can avoid this problem by checking what color is wanting to come through you, what tone or emotion wants a voice in your life. Here are some things you can do to determine what color is seeking your attention.

At the end of every month, do a meditation and ask your soul to give you a color you need to focus on. Of all psychic impressions, colors are the easiest to receive. Wait until you are feeling relaxed inside before you ask for the color, until your mind is clear and open to guidance.

After the meditation, write briefly about what the color means to you, and how you should integrate it into your life. Write quickly and without thought.

> *Blue is the color of my sadness. I need to cry more, to take some walks alone on the beach and talk to my dead father. He is calling me. He wants to help me. I miss him . . .*

Be your own guide. Let the color give you a personal reading.

Every once in a while, examine your clothes closet to see if you have been drawn to any new colors. If you have, pursue some activities that correspond to the colors to which you are attracted. For example, in a red year, I bought two burgundy T-shirts, a scarlet blazer, and some cherry-colored surf shorts. By looking in my closet, I knew that it was time to turn on my wildness. The color red acted as a guide, showing me what part of myself I was longing to express.

If you have outgrown some of the shades of your wardrobe, move on. Put an end to your pastel skirts or gray blazers and buy an outfit in a color that is calling you. You will be amazed how good it feels to dress in accordance with your inner being.

Think about the landscapes you've been craving. In a violet phase, you might have the desire to visit temples and spiritual bookstores. In an orange phase, you might want to go dancing, or stay home in bed with your lover watching reruns of *Mork and Mindy*. Go where you're being called, where you can jump into the color and experience it with total abandon.

As I tell my students, in order to live our true lives, we must develop our entire being, activate all the dormant colors in our body. These practices I just mentioned will help you stay on track.

⊚ Reading the Colors Outside You

You can use your color awareness externally, to get a deeper view of a person's character or see into a future situation. Here are some techniques I use in my daily life to guide myself and others on their soul's path.

Close your eyes and tune in to the presence of a friend or even a person you have just met. They don't have to be in the same room with you. They could be in another city or across the dinner table. Follow the same steps you did in the first exercise on receiving colors, only this time you will be reading the colors in his magnetic field rather than a color being projected to you. It is the same process. Let your whole body be a receiver, seeing this person from the bones all the way to the edge of his aura.

If you are doing the exercise with a friend, share with him what you think the colors mean, information his soul is trying to pass on that perhaps he is not hearing. I did this exercise with my wife and my friend Wesley on a street corner one night in Santa Monica. We stood in a triangle and read each other's colors while people were passing by us on the sidewalk. I learned from that night that it is best to speak while your eyes are closed, so that your words fuse together with your observation, rather than viewing and speaking separately. It's like calling your mother on the telephone from Hawaii and describing a sunset to her as it's happening. Certain levels of awareness need to be mentioned in the moment, or else they are lost.

If you are doing this exercise with a stranger—someone you don't feel comfortable enough to read in person—write down everything you feel, and refer to it later on, after you know him or her better, to see where your insights were accurate. Remember, seeing a color will awaken new brain cells, causing unexpected ideas to flow through your pen. Don't censor yourself. Let the color push you into new frontiers of writing, new depths of speech.

If you have a big date coming up, or an important meeting, try opening yourself to the situation before it happens; visualize in your body the colors you need to be in touch with to experience the event with total aliveness.

I do this sometimes before I go to work in the Hollywood restaurant where I give readings. I sit quietly in my office or car and do a viewing of the restaurant to see what the dominant color of the evening will be. It's like watching the weather channel before a camping trip. If I see white, then I know I will be invited to rise to some higher elevation, maybe speak with a guide or a dead relative. Knowing this, I can begin my ascent at home, do some prayer work and mantras, so that by the time I get to work I will be cruising at the right altitude.

If I see red, I can take some time to awaken my animal body, perhaps have a cold shower, dance to some drum music, or do some fast breathing exercises to stimulate my instincts.

Being succesful in the world requires that we constantly fine-tune ourselves, to keep our magnetic fields ready for the challenges of the day. When you know the general color of an event ahead of time, the curve balls don't throw you so much.

There are many colors I didn't write about in this chapter, such as pink, black, magenta, brown, and turquoise. They, too, can appear in the human aura. If I left out one of your special colors, research it in other books, or write a poem on what the color means to you. The seven I mentioned can blend together into infinite patterns. Trust your instincts. At a soul level, we all know what a color means.

Seeing the Buddha

The past is in our midst, waiting to be touched with new eyes.

 In today's culture, we are taught we can visit history only through vehicles like books, movies, or paintings; that the past is, for the most part, a locked file. Through exploring my seer abilities, I no longer accept this as true. It started when I took up poetry in my early teens. I'd be sitting at my desk writing some verses about a long-ago time, and my brain would flash like a movie screen and receive a flood of impressions that were as real to me as memories.

Years later, when I became a psychic, the visionary states I encountered were exactly the same. When I saw a fragment of my client's past, it came to me with the same shimmering radiance as the images I contacted with my pen. There was no difference. My imagination had become a tool of seeing. I learned that it is just as easy to witness an event from three hundred years ago—a nasty king pacing the halls of his castle—as it is to remember a scene from our childhood. Our souls have a link with all the memories of the world. All we have to do is focus our attention and be still, and the past steps forward into the present.

Although few of them claim to be seers, many authors and filmmakers who use historical themes in their work experience this inner time travel. Novelist Taylor Caldwell said that while writing her stories about the Roman Empire and Ancient Greece, she had real visions, like memories, of having lived in those times and being intimately connected with many of the characters she was writing about. In a sense, she was writing about her own past, a past she had lived in another body.

Paleontologists also use the seer in their work. Reconstructing an extinct species requires a great deal of inner seeing. Scientists are probably the last people on earth to admit to being engaged in a psychic art, but it only makes sense that the intensity of their research would invoke visionary perceptions, actual viewings of what the world looked like when dinosaurs roamed the earth.

In old times, imagination and reality were partners. What was seen in dreams and meditations was just as valid as what was read in a scroll. Nowadays they are enemies. We give credit to what is observed through a microscope and discount what is seen by the soul. Of course, we must possess some kind of internal screening device to weed out superstitious impressions (not everyone was Cleopatra in a past life) but not something so dense that we discredit our personal visions of the past, our ancestors.

In my workshops, I do an exercise called "Seeing the Buddha." It is based on the party game, *If you could have dinner with anyone from the past, who would it be?* The exercise is designed to help people let go of their limited view of time, to open their sight to an individual from the past, and receive a photographic view of his or her life.

Rather than having my students focus on just anyone, I have them select what I call a "holy person." When I say holy, I don't mean a religious figure, but anyone who led a soulful life, gave humanity something inspiring to remember. From this perspective you might include Rimbaud, Sappho, or Einstein. It is better to focus on a holy person than a tyrant, because then the exercise will feed you rather than sap you, drawing into your body some of the enlightened material that passed through their lives.

If there is no one in history that meets your definition of holiness, you can view a mythological character instead: Zeus, Aphrodite, Merlin, Krishna. They are just as real and open to contact as someone who lived in a body. If you don't believe me, give it a try.

Here's how the ritual works.

Step one. Sit in a circle with one or more persons and jointly select a holy person from the past you wish to explore. Once you have made your selection, everyone in the circle close their eyes, hold hands, and begin your viewing. Use the same method you applied when receiving colors. Let your whole body take in the impressions, from your neocortex to your toenails. Breathe slowly. Relax.

If it helps, visualize yourself opening an invisible book of history, an encyclopedia of all the great beings who walked the earth . . . or as in the Superman movie, imagine a memory crystal entering your heart, containing vital scenes from the character's life . . . whatever stimulates your vision.

In one of my classes, two students did a viewing of Gandhi. One woman saw him in a garden, digging his hands into the earth, with a fierce concentration in his eyes, as if nothing existed but the plants and vegetables in front of him. Her partner received an image of Gandhi walking with a crowd of people down an abandoned road. She said there was a light surrounding him that was irresistible, that made you want to drop everything you were doing and travel beside him. Not only did she contact Gandhi's essence, but she was also fed by the vision, given a rich memory to return to in difficult times.

If you feel for some reason that you are not seeing a real event, that it is just your imagination operating the camera and not the seer, still allow yourself to embrace the experience. In such a ritual, our imagination is usually not that far off. It might embellish or idealize the subject matter, but the energy behind the images will still be authentic. In a psychic landscape, you can't always judge the book by the cover. Sometimes the feeling is more important than the picture.

When my friend John did a viewing of Christ, he saw many scenes of anger and outrage. He had expected to receive impressions of Christ the healer, Christ with light in his hands curing a band of lepers. He didn't expect to be drawn to the human side of Christ, the man who felt the energy of the heavens and wanted everyone else to follow his way. The seer will take you to the side of the person you need to see. Be open. Let yourself feel the pulse of their heart.

Step two. After five or ten minutes of viewing, go around the circle and share your impressions, what you saw, felt, discovered. Discuss areas of agreement, contradiction, insight. Even though you are no longer in meditation, the presence you contacted is still with you, still running through your body. Feel the person as you are speaking. Let him or her inspire your words.

If you are in the mood, select another person and begin again. If you are a beginner, it might take a few tries to break in. At first, you might only get small bites, but in time, the exercise will become more profound. The residue of your viewing will stay with you all day. You will feel Gandhi beside you as you push your shopping cart down the grocery aisle, or see Aphrodite's glowing skin on the face of your lover.

In my classes, I act as the tour guide. I say a prayer to sanctify the atmosphere, to get everyone relaxed and open. If there is someone in your group who could take on this role—say a few warm words before the ritual begins—it will make the viewing more vibrant.

I also like to talk to the person before I visit them. I say something like this, "Buddha, we would like to see your world, to watch you as you were when you were alive. We wish to know your life, to be a part of your teachings. Reveal yourself to us. Let us be one with your being . . ."

Once you get well practiced at this exercise, you can use it in your daily life. If your friends are having a conversation on a historical subject about which you have no knowledge—a famous leader, a war, an extinct species—you can turn inside and check your own resources, do a quick viewing to see what images and sensations come into your mind.

Some people might think you're nuts, to make comments about Napoleon or Nero based on your own internal sources, but who cares? Fifty years from now, it will be much different. The inner libraries will be just as respected at the public ones. I have seen it in my meditations. The soul will once again be the ultimate authority.

If you have a strong skeptical side as I do, go and research your impressions to see how far off you were, and where you hit the bull's-eye. As my friend Pendragon Hoff said, most of what we read about the past is gossip, hand-me-down information from biased historians. Using the seer might be the only chance we have to see what really happened, to know our ancestors from the inside out; in the heart and soul, rather than just dates, costumes, and worldly achievements.

Have fun. The entire history of the world is at your disposal.

Seeing Jane

I shut my eyes in order to see.
—Paul Gaugin

 There are moments in our lives when we wish we could be closer to the people we love, slip out of our skin and enter a more intimate field of space. The poets of the nineteenth century expressed this longing all the time. *I want to melt into you, pour my essence down your sleeves . . .*

As a species, we have in many ways betrayed our need for psychic closeness. We have chosen isolation over community, replaced our intuitive connection with phone lines and Internet services, made our bodies afraid of intimacy, our minds resistant to merging.

Fortunately, there are people who still live the old way, who know how to link souls, to meet in spirit as lovers do in the body. In meditation, my mother had a vision of a group of Aborigines who were gifted seers, able to reach their eyes across space and touch the core of another being. She saw them in the forest, sitting around a large fire, speaking without words. Currents of energy united the members of the tribe at the forehead and the heart, enabling them to send each other pure transmissions of feeling and thought. They lived as one being, one mechanism of light.

When you call the seer into your life, this is what happens. The aching separation between you and your friends, your spouse, your dead loved ones, begins to disappear. Slowly you start to inhabit a larger body, feeling with your eyes the web of energy that holds us all together.

When we unite in vision, our power increases. We can summon forces significant enough to have a healing impact on the entire world. My mother told me that the Aborigines are doing this right now, using their visionary abilities to help humanity attune themselves to a higher awareness, so that we can move into the millennium gracefully, without a glow of radiation hovering above our heads. If there is such a thing as prayer, this is it.

I have devised a ritual that will teach you how to achieve this psychic closeness with the ones you love, and strengthen your inner sight. I call it "Seeing Jane." I chose this title because it is conventional, prosaic. For too long psychic awareness has been kept in a vault, wrapped in gold paper, forbidden to the masses. Living as a seer is not like this. It's about seeing heaven in ordinary things, feeling a relationship with all of life, from the grasshopper and the lily to the Wall Street tycoon.

In order to do this ritual well, you need another person, a friend who is open, trustworthy, and cares for your well-being. If you don't have such a friend, call one into your life. Two years ago I had no men with whom I was close, only women—my wife, my mother, my sister, a few female friends. I was starving for male companionship. One afternoon, I got down on my knees and cried out to my soul to send me some real friends, guys I could share my feelings with, who wouldn't be afraid to walk through the fire, shed tears, read poetry.

That year they all arrived, five of them, like lost brothers coming home after a long voyage. If you don't have close friends, pray them into your life. I promise you, they will come. If you shout loud enough, they will hear your call.

Step one. Invite your friend to set aside time each week where you will practice seeing each other, and reporting your visions. In the late afternoon or early evening, do a viewing of your friend's day, observing what has happened since the morning until now. In the same manner you saw the holy person, see your friend. Go into meditation. Use your inner sight.

When you focus in, begin by asking simple questions. How is my friend doing today? Is he joyful, melancholy, magical, confused?

What is his mood, his state of mind? Wait a second to see what happens, what images come pulsing into your mind. Track any new sensations in your body: a sore stomach, stiff shoulders, a dry mouth, glowing genitals.

Write your impressions down in your notebook and then tune in again, this time asking more specific questions. What is my friend wearing? Who is he with? What did he eat for breakfast? What color are his shoes?

Step two. After a ten- or fifteen-minute viewing, call your friend and share what you saw. As Judith Orloff says in her book *Second Sight*, "Feedback is central to developing as a psychic." Tell your friend everything that came to you. If you received a picture of her being devoured by a giant cat, say it. She might have had a fight with her boss, taken a trip to the zoo, watched a rerun of a Tarzan movie. Sometimes our abstract impressions carry the most accuracy. It might take a few minutes or weeks for them to make sense, but they are usually right on the money. Be wild. Don't hold back.

Caution: In the beginning, your mind might play tricks on you. Every time you tune into your friend, you might see her wearing garter belts or a cowboy hat, or swimming in a fish bowl. Keep trying. After a while, you will be able to tell the difference between what is imaginary and what is real. You will feel it in your gut.

If a playful image persists, write a story or poem about it. Give it some movement, a place to exist. A lot of us neglect our imagination. To appear mature and wise, we tape the child's mouth, hold down our whimsical urges. In such rituals, the parts of you that have been suppressed will want to speak. Don't let the good stuff get away. Take the pictures you receive and make them into art.

Whenever you get stuck in this ritual, ask questions and take slow, deep breaths. During the early stages of psychic development, you might have to find a quiet room to perform your talents, unplug the phone, turn off the television. After a while, however, you will not need a formal atmosphere to activate your seeing. These instincts will become a seamless part of your life.

Step three. After you alternate three or four times with your friend, come together and do an Aborigine ritual. Sit across from each other and imagine a beam of light connecting you at the third eye and the heart. This time, don't say anything. Don't give any reports. Just tune in to each other for fifteen or twenty minutes, and watch the impressions flow through your head. This will help you establish a psychic bond with the person that will give your next viewings more accuracy. When you call each other the following week, you will feel more connected. Coming together and meditating is a way of tuning up, keeping the line between you clear and vital.

In the next part of the book, "Awakening the Empath," there will be rituals to take you a step further into the art of interconnectedness. You will learn how to surrender your heart to true companionship, to give yourself over to a complete psychic relationship. In any metaphysical practice, this is the primary study—learning how to be intimate with other beings, to sink into the essential reality where there exists a pathway of communication between all living things.

When we activate the seer, our eyes start to sew the world together, bringing all of our perceptions into a single tapestry.

Seeing Another Place

The geography of this room, I know so well tonight.
—MICHAEL ONDAATJE

 Like a cinematographer, the seer can film either fiction or reality, can flash into our mind an imaginary love scene or an actual moment of combat from the Vietnam War. Most of us don't know this. We think a psychic uses a different set of eyes, that our daydreams of Tahiti are not as vibrant as what the card reader sees when she closes her eyes. The truth is, they are both the same. The flights of imagination you have while sitting on the subway are as much the work of the seer as the visions Nostradamus had meditating in his cellar. The equipment doesn't change. It's the intention, the way it's used. We are creatures of light. We see. It's our nature.

In my workshops, rather than exploring fantasy realms (which people do quite well on their own), I invite my students to use their sight to view a place that is real—not just a person, but an environment, a human dwelling filled with memories, sofas, pets, cooking smells. For some reason, when you view a three-dimensional space, your senses come alive. There is something about walking around in your mind, turning down hallways, opening doors, that awakens your vision. It's like those interactive adventure games where you roll dice and enter mythical landscapes: cross a moat, descend into a pit, fly into the ether on a prehistoric bird. The seer is a traveler. With movement, she can record more details.

Viewing another person's home also teaches you how to track energy fields, tap into the mood of a room, and diagnose subtle conditions. It's important to be able to sense danger zones, places where your body isn't comfortable; or as my wife does, select the table in the restaurant that will inspire the most enjoyable conversation. Knowing these things not only makes you happier, but can also save your life.

Step one. Sit with a partner and have her visualize in her mind one of the houses she lived in growing up, one you never visited. If you've been best friends since grade one, and have seen every house she lived in, have her visualize a relative's home, a holiday cabin, or an office where she worked. Anywhere you haven't been.

When you're ready, turn inside and begin to walk through the house. Start at the front door. Knock if you want. Pretend you are the Avon Lady going inside to have a cup of tea and show off your new lipsticks. Sometimes these gimmicks work, disarming the mind into revealing its powers.

Be present with all your senses. What do you smell baking in the oven? What music is playing? Is it a two-story house? Is the furniture bright or dark? What is the emotional feeling of the residence?

When your mind goes blank, return to simple observations. Am I hot or cold? Happy or sad? Is there a dog in the house? A bird? Are there trees at the window?

Report all your impressions to your partner. When you are off, don't get discouraged. Keep sniffing around, walking into new rooms, down stairs, through doors. Ask your partner questions when you get stuck. Play the hot and cold game. If you are the person who is thinking of the space, say the words "warm" or "cold" to give direction. Be nice. Give clues.

In one workshop I conducted, a woman came to a closet in the kitchen that she did not want to enter; she told me she sensed something painful in there that would weaken her if she came too close. I stopped the exercise and invited Laura, the girl who had lived in the house, to enter the closet. Without hesitation, she said yes.

After she visualized herself climbing into the dark space, I told

Laura to ask who was hiding in there. I could feel the presence of someone in the closet, a lonely person needing help. It turned out that the resident of the closet was one year old. When she asked who it was, she heard her own name.

Communicating with the child revealed to Laura many insights about her past. As a baby, she had felt as if she had landed in the wrong home. No one in her family was able to communicate with her on the level she needed. Her parents had no soul life. The residue of this pain was still in her body. She had a lump in her throat, and could speak only in a polite, whispery voice. In order to protect herself, Laura had become withdrawn and timid. She kept her real self hidden for fear that she would be laughed at or ignored. The closet was not a real closet, but a metaphor of an enclosed personality, an infant who had not received the proper love.

As she talked with the child, the room was electric. She was not the only one who was giving the baby support. The entire class was in loving correspondence with this scared one-year-old. I had not planned for us to go into this vulnerable place. We were led there by a higher force, a collective need to heal the fear and loneliness stored in our bodies.

With this exercise, you can be scanning the surface and, without knowing it, penetrate into a deep vein of feeling. As the old expression goes, home is where the heart is. Aside from the tables and chairs and baseball trophies, a home contains all the trauma and intimate stories of the people who live there. When you are walking through the house, remember this. Allow yourself to sink into the carpets, breathe in the walls, touch the rich layer of memories stored in everything you see.

If by chance your partner finds something or someone from the past who is calling you, switch sides and go check it out. Talk to a lost child, adult, or pet, as if they were in the room with you. Don't worry about applying a technique. Just be natural. Shine your light where it is needed.

Usually we have to be ten or fifteen years past the hurt to have the strength and insight to go back and heal it. If you can remember a room or a house that you lived in that was a capsule of grief, where you suffered great loss or sorrow, do a viewing on your own. Use your sight to venture inward to set free the part of yourself that is still trapped there, preventing you from living your soul's path. Light a candle, close your eyes, and go and talk to the hurt part of you that is stuck in the past. Expect a lot of tears when you touch these hidden spaces, and a lot of growth.

For fun, you can use this exercise to look into places that you might never get to visit: the Taj Mahal, the Tower of London, the tomb of King Tut, the space shuttle. Again, if you are skeptical, go research your visions. See if they were true.

After doing the exercise with your friend, try to become more aware of physical spaces. Examine how certain cafés affect you, where you feel like walking in a bookstore, what spot in the house is the most peaceful, what table you are drawn to in a restaurant. Be you own Feng Shui designer. Place vases and photographs not only where they look good, but also where it feels right. Lie on the carpet more. Look at things from new perspectives.

Start living like a cat, intensely aware of your environment, from the wind ripples on the curtain, to the amber light emanating from your lover's hands. Our attention increases over time. When you are ready to see more, you will. Start by appreciating what is visible, and the invisible will mysteriously reveal itself.

Signs

Everything is part of it.
—TOM ROBBINS

 Many diseases, accidents, premature deaths, are the result of people having lost the ability to read signs, both in their bodies and the external world. Since we moved out of the wilderness—where sign reading is an absolute must if you wish to survive—we have become less aware of when our soul is speaking to us through our physical environment. We have to develop a new style of sign reading, to connect ourselves with a mythology that often feels artificial and nonliving.

In my teens, I read a lot of contemporary poets; Allen Ginsberg, Charles Bukowski, Wanda Coleman, Richard Brautigan. Because they included a lot of modern images in their poems, they helped me connect with the "signs of the time," to feel an instinctual relationship with the inorganic materials of the twentieth century. After absorbing their words, I no longer felt I was living in the wrong era. I started to see soul in everything around me. I didn't need to go back in time. I could stay right where I was.

This is the first step in learning how to read signs. You must see the sacred in all levels of matter, from a hummingbird, all the way to a rusty crowbar, a coffee cup, a drunk on the street. When we lived in the jungle, we couldn't afford to disregard anything. Even a tiny insect could be a messenger, bringing us a sign of some natural disaster that was headed our way. Things haven't changed. If you are open, the whole world can be your guide.

A lot of the sign reading we do each day comes from experience, common sense, habit. We see dark clouds in the sky and predict that rain is coming. We notice clothing and appliances lying on our neighbor's lawn, and assume they are having a yard sale.

There are other signs we receive that are less rational, signs the seer slips us at the oddest moments with a specific message just for us. You could be reading a magazine and a word from a perfume ad jumps out at you, reminding you to meet with your lawyer. You could pass a coffee shop on your way to work that triggers a wave of longing for an old college friend, and when you call her that night, you find out her mother just died.

Signs are everywhere. If you are observant, you can receive them all the time. The way the stoplight blinks, the chair your cat sits on when he enters the room, the color of the flower your child brings you home from school. The most ordinary events can provide you with a message, an intuitive cue to keep you on course and prepare you for what is going to happen next.

As the Buddhists say, the world is empty. We are the ones who fill it up. The art of reading signs comes from extracting images in our environment that mirror our intuition. The messages really come from inside us. If you view it the other way around, that objects are personally speaking to you, you might lose your mind. As you walk through the supermarket, oranges will start singing to you, soup cans calling your name.

Be alert to signs, but don't let them control you. You are the master, the seer, the mystic. Signs are just your inner voice appearing in the things around you.

◎ Decoding Signs

If your attention fixes on something you think is a sign, and you don't know what it means, ask the seer to interpret it for you. Close you eyes for a second and wait for some inner clue, a voice, a picture, a sound. If you still feel stuck, write something about it. Turn to a blank page in your journal and just let your pen flow. If it was a tree that spoke to you, do a quick word association.

Hold the image of the tree in your consciousness and write down every other word that comes into your mind. Then look at the page to see if there is a pattern, a message that stands out.

Our souls are often trying to communicate something to us about our inner life. As humans, we are usually pretty good with worldly pursuits: career, bills, shopping. Where we most frequently go astray is with our spiritual work. A tree might simply be a sign that we need to slow down, rest, meditate, breathe, paint. Sometimes it's that simple.

◉ Signs of Synchronicity

There are moments in our life when we are acting in such perfect harmony with our soul, that a sign will appear in the outer world to bless our actions. You could be in a field painting, and a raven will cry at the top of his lungs, signaling to you that you are working on a piece of sacred art. You might receive a sign when you're talking with a stranger in line at the bank. A car alarm will start ringing at the same time as you introduce yourselves, affirming that the chemistry you feel for the person is genuine, and that you should get his number before you part ways.

When I am doing readings in the restaurant, I receive these kinds of signs all the time. A leaf will fall onto the table when I enter a crucial section of a client's reading. A waiter will drop a plate when I make an accurate prediction. Sometimes a sign has a specific message, and sometimes it is just there to make you feel good, to remind you that you are not alone, that a higher intelligence is presiding over the chaos of the world, and you are in tune with it.

One of the most beautiful signs I've ever received came to me while I was sitting with a few buddies in the park discussing relationships—especially the difficulty men have in choosing between a life of prolonged bachelorhood or intimate marriage. My friend had just separated from his girlfriend, and was torn over whether or not he should celebrate his new freedom, or go out and buy an engagement ring. During a moment of silence, two monarch butterflies flew between us, spiraling up and down in the air like flirting lovers. Nature was showing us a model of how two creatures can be together and not interfere with each other's flight.

The sign took us a step deeper into the heart. Another force had joined our conversation. We all smiled with delight.

If you want to explore a synchronistic sign on a more intimate level, focus on it in meditation. Sit quietly at home and tune your mind to the moment the sign happened. Feel in your body the electrical charge that passed through you as you realized the sign was for you. Enter into that grid of consciousness and allow your intuition to feed you more messages.

At the moment of receiving a sign, our antennae are fully alert, like a pole being zapped with lightning. Meditating on these moments will make you more psychic; it will train the seer in you to pick up the most sensitive signals.

⚙ Asking for Signs

As we are moving through the day, often we need some quick guidance to help us stay on track, and don't know how to get it. We could be talking on the phone with a client, walking through a foreign city, driving home late at night, and out of the blue, require a dose of higher advice . . . a sign from the gods. Here's something you can do in these desperate times, to keep you in contact with the seer. It's a fun exercise that has worked wonders for me in the most stressful moments.

First off, wherever you are, turn inside yourself and focus on the issue that is perplexing you. Breathe slowly. Let it pulse through your body. The issue could be about anything: whether or not to buy an expensive pair of sunglasses, visit a certain doctor, confront your friend about his abusive humor. The sign will help you know if it is the right time, whether you should act now, or wait for a better moment.

When you feel ready, scan your environment and track the first thing that really grabs your attention—a lamp, an apple, a billboard. Without any mental interference, let your intuition tell you what the object means, what message it is carrying in response to your problem.

At first this might feel like a silly thing to do. Your eyes will engage an object, and your mind will be blank, confused. You will laugh at yourself for having tried to seek wisdom from a chair or a glass of water. I felt this when I started reading Tarot cards. In the beginning, they were just a jumble of shapes, pictures, symbols. My eyes were unable to sniff out messages for me, focus in on an image and draw out a specific insight.

Activating the seer takes practice, an open mind, and a childlike willingness to experiment and have fun. If you do this exercise a few times a day, soon you will be able to read signs in the subtlest details—pens, doorknobs, tiepins, potted plants. Your soul will be able to reach you during a business meeting, a date, or an exam, giving you guidance with a simple movement of your eyes.

Years and years ago, before we read books and shopped at 7-Eleven, this mode of sign reading was instinctual. The world spoke to us all the time. We asked it questions. It replied. And on we went. To get back this psychic relationship, we need to work a little bit, to go through some awkward steps to reharmonize ourselves with the wisdom of matter.

As I was writing this section of the chapter, I asked the seer to give me a sign, a message for how I should compose this exercise so that you, the reader, won't think it's crazy to receive guidance from inorganic objects. Immediately my eyes locked onto the lamp on my desk. Intuitively, I heard the word "light" in my head. The seer was advising me to keep it light, simple, clear, funny. Even as I write this now, I am learning more about what the lamp meant. It is still speaking to me. The signs we get from our soul can be traveled into as deeply as we want. I could keep writing about the lamp, and receive more and more messages, enough to fill a few pages of this book. Sometimes this happens to me in a reading. I stay locked on the same image for fifteen minutes, mesmerized by reels of information. Signs are gateways, openings into alternate universes. You can keep sinking, keep exploring, until you find exactly what you want.

Learning this skill of reading signs will assist you in other modes of divination, such as Rune stones, Tarot cards, or Yarrow sticks. In order to use these systems well, you need to go beyond surface definitions and interpret the meaning of the moment, that which has never been said before. With a sign, there are no guidebooks to follow. All you have is an image and your intuition.

Most of us have forgotten that this life is an adventure, a riddle, a myth. We will spend hours playing Myst on our computer, decoding enigmatic symbols to solve the game, but we won't give our own journey the same attention. Watching for signs is a way of honoring the fact that we are travelers, seekers, searching for our own holy grail. It makes our lives more real.

One last suggestion. Each day when you wake up in the morning, ask your soul to send you three signs that will give you guidance—clear, intelligible signs. It will make the day magical and multilayered. When you get the sign, you'll feel your insides ring with achievement, because you created it. The sign was your creation.

After a while, you will feel as though you are living in two worlds at once. Before a storm happens, you will be able to send out a lifeboat to rescue yourself. This is the way an advanced soul lives, with two or three glasses always chilled in the freezer, awaiting interesting guests.

The Art of
Prediction

Billy Pilgrim says that the Universe does not look like a
series of bright dots to the creatures from Tralfamadore.
The creatures can see where each star has been and where
it is going, so that the heavens are filled with rarefied,
luminous spaghetti. And Tralfamadorians don't see human
beings as two-legged creatures, either. They see them
as great millipedes—with babies' legs at one end and old
people's legs at the other . . .

—KURT VONNEGUT

 Predicting the future is an ordinary part of our daily
lives. We do it all the time, in subtle ways, often without
even realizing we did it. In most of us, the seer is an
unconscious force, the hero who saves the day and
leaves no fingerprints. Seconds before the pasta boils onto the
stove, something will guide us to the kitchen to turn off the flame.
We'll accidentally exit at the wrong street and miss a deadly accident. On a whim, we'll select the long shot at a horse race and
win a thousand dollars. Impulsively, we'll wear red to an audition,
and find out later on that it's the director's favorite color.

Almost everyone I've met tells me they've had moments of
prophecy. Mothers especially have this gift. In the early years of
childhood, a mother probably makes a hundred accurate predictions that save her child's life. Same with police officers. They use
foresight all the time. It's part of the job. Not only does their
flashlight extend into the shadows, but so does their mind.

Prediction carries the Indo-European root word *deik*, which
means to teach, to pronounce solemnly, to wiggle your finger and
point. This mode of seeing has been with us since the beginning
of time. In Ancient Rome, the ruling class used predictions from

the oracles to help govern the state, fight wars, build new cities. The Chinese had advanced systems of prediction, from the *I Ching* to the fortune cookie. I'm sure that even cavemen made predictions, that a woman would wake her husband early in the morning, point in the direction of a certain line of hills, and say, "Go there . . . good hunting . . . big mammoth waiting for you at three o'clock . . ."

Prediction is not a black art, as many Christians believe, but rather a natural function of the psyche, as important to our survival as breathing and sleeping. There are times when we just absolutely need to know what is going to happen next, what shape and size of wave is going to hit our boat. Animals make predictions all the time. When a squirrel stores nuts at the end of summer, he is following an instinctual rhythm, a predictive coding in his cells that tells him winter is on its way.

Prediction is the opposite of remembering. When you make a prediction, you jump forward in time rather than backward. As children (before grown-ups told us that humans can't see the future), we had memories not only of the past, but also of what lay ahead, many years down the road. I've had numerous *déjà vu* experiences when I realized that the child in me had seen this moment a long time ago. When I met my wife, I felt like this all the time. I felt like Chuang-Tzu; I didn't know if I was a man dreaming of himself as a child, or a child dreaming of himself as a man. When we are young, our daydreams often tapped into a realm of prediction. Without knowing it, we uncovered scenes of our adult life. A game of dress-up became a sacred ritual, a journey into the future.

Although they use different words to describe their process, most artists are masters of prediction. A screenwriter friend says that when he writes a script, he views scenes ahead of time, catching glimpses of the second act while he is still laboring on the first. I am sure wizards like Mozart experienced this all the time. While he was laying down the opening notes of his concerto, part of his awareness was probably already at the end of the composition, sensing the final rush of violins, the last breath of flutes.

No matter how accurate a prediction is, there is still mystery. The seer reveals only parts of the story. We still must make our voyage into the unknown. Be skeptical of psychics who predict the future as if they were a mouthpiece of God. The future is not written in stone. The slightest shift in our awareness can set us off in a new direction. A prediction is like a weather forecast. It is possible that what appears like thunder showers today will be nothing but sunny skies tomorrow, or the other way around, depending on how the gods are feeling . . .

◎ All Time Is Now

As Einstein discovered, all time is now. Events from our childhood and old age circulate through our bodies like a network of rivers. In meditation, you can actually feel trails of experience pouring outward from your heart into other stages of your life, hear voices passing to and fro, from the five-year-old child all the way to the laughing elder.

In *Letters to a Young Poet*, Rilke talks about how shocked people are when their destiny appears, as if they never saw it coming. He says that it is not meant to be this way, that if we are conscious of what is growing inside us, the future is quite obvious. An apple doesn't just suddenly appear on the tree. Nature moves slowly, in cycles. Seeds are planted long before the harvest.

In order to know how the future is moving within us, Rilke advises us to not run away from our times of sadness, but to stay with our heavy feelings and follow them to their roots. "The more still, more patient and more open we are when we are sad, so much the deeper, and so much the more unswervingly does the new go into us, so much the better do we make it ours, so much the more will it be our destiny. And when on some later day it happens (that is, steps forth out of us to others), we shall feel in our inmost selves akin and near to it."

As well as being a great seer, Rilke was also a great listener. Most of his poems are set with a tone of rich inward attention. He knew what type of storm was coming by the size of raindrops that touched his skin. His writing is not about straight lines. It carries the arcs and circles of the seer, casting out predictions in many directions at once.

By simply observing what is passing through your inner world, you can uncover a great deal of information about your future. Before reading any further, write down in your notebook all the new qualities you've been feeling in yourself over the last year, and where you think they are leading you.

For example, if you are feeling a new shade of humor growing inside you, in what way do you think it will be expressed down the road? Is there a play you are going to write? Is it drawing toward you a new group of eccentric friends?

Maybe you've become more assertive lately, more daring in conversation. Where will this shift take you? Will it lead you to a new job? A new book? A new lover? A role in politics?

When you catch something in its seedling form, you can have more control over how it develops, giving it the proper nutrients, and the best angle of sunlight. As Rilke said, our future doesn't have to shock us; we can be creatively involved with our destiny.

Remember, prediction comes from being aware of what is happening in the subtle layers of your being, what embryos are spinning into form. Through practices such as meditation, journal writing, and breath work, you can begin to get in tune with the rhythms of your body, become conscious of the steps that need to take place in order for you to give birth to a new experience.

You will also learn how to break the shell of dark emotions, so that healthy stems may rise to the surface and feed your future. Many great books were written in a depression, many great campaigns fought with childhood anger. Whatever is inside you right now is there for a reason. See what it wants to tell you, where it is leading you on your soul's path.

◎ A Few Methods to Enhance Your Predictive Ability

Prediction Journal

Keep a journal in the house in which you catalog your predictions. Whenever you get a feeling of something that is going to happen—either to you, a friend, or even the world—write it down. List the date and time the prediction came to you, and also a few notes about how your were feeling, what emotions were running through you when the prediction entered your mind.

Sometimes we make a negative prediction because we are feeling lousy. After a fight with our spouse, we might have the feeling the whole world is going to blow up, or that an earthquake is going to destroy the city. If you write down some notes, you will soon know if it is your soul or a bad mood that is sending you the prediction.

Trying to place a date on your prediction of the future is optional because it is very tricky. What feels like a year away could happen tomorrow. As Edgar Cayce scholar Mark Thurston writes in *Millennium Prophecies:* "Predictions require the seer to operate in a dimension of consciousness that is beyond the normal constraints of time and space, but then to articulate his visions in terms of a specific time frame." In a prediction, time is secondary. What you see is more important.

Remember, be descriptive when you make your predictions. If you engage your creative mind, the seer will tell you more as you are writing.

> *At three o'clock today, as I was reading an article in the* Times *about union strikes, I had a vision of a new cat coming into my life, a fluffy white Persian. When I saw the cat, my body trembled. I think I will meet the cat in the next six months.*

If you want, you can also keep a bowl in the kitchen just for monthly predictions. Every time you sit down to pay your bills, you can read last month's predictions and make a few new ones. This is a great exercise for children, to get the seer speaking in their lives. It's like making your own fortune cookies, for you and the family.

Remembering Past Predictions

Make a list of all the predictions you've made in your life, from the tiny and absurd, to the huge and marvelous. Retrieve the memory of how you felt when each prediction entered you. What were you doing? What state of mind were you in? What bodily sensations were going on?

If you think you're one of those people who's never made a prediction, think again. We've all had moments of foresight, knowing ahead of time what dress our mother would wear to dinner, who would win the football game, how long it would take to buy our first house. We can't stop our psyche from seeing the future. Our vision has no choice but to look ahead.

Also, whenever you are feeling cut off from your soul, psychically inert, meditate on one of your favorite predictive moments. It will be like putting on an old pair of glasses. Your inner sight will be restored. You will see again!

Predicting with Hands

Not only can you make a prediction from a person's palm, in the traditional gypsy manner, but you can also read the future by holding someone's hand. I learned this technique from my brother George. It is a kind of prayer, a way of sharing deep insights from one body to another.

Here's how you do it.

Sit with a friend in a quiet place, take her hand in yours, and close your eyes. Breathe. Open yourself to the currents of energy running between you. When you feel relaxed, ask the seer to show you something about her future. Since you are touching her, the pictures you receive will be more immediate, rushing into your mind like electricity through a plug. Speak the images at the exact moment they come to you, with no hesitation, as if you were dictating a movie to a blind person.

This is what my brother said in the first reading he gave me:

> *Andrei, I see you sitting on a red stage with a guitar on your lap. You are in an old theater, with a kind of Gothic feeling to it. There are about five hundred people in the audience. You are alone on stage: just you, a chair, and a microphone. You are dressed in a black suit, and look about forty years old. The music is pouring out of you. You are very happy.*

Since I got the reading, this image has appeared in my mind at least a hundred times. I have always had a lot of doubts about my ability to succeed as a musician. George's prediction is like a confidence pill; it helps me believe in the reality of my dreams.

When you do this exercise, ask the seer to give you and your friend inspiring visions. When we humans know there is light in our future, it gives us strength to create more. Having a picture in our mind of where we are going is half the battle of getting there.

Fun Predictions

During the day there are a lot of opportunities to make fun predictions. On our way to work, we can predict what color of tie our boss is going to be wearing. Before our children go on a field trip to the zoo, we can predict what their favorite animal will be. We can predict some of the items in our friend's refrigerator before we open it, what the weather will be like on Tuesday, how much in tips we'll make on the lunch shift, how many home runs our team will score, what color of underwear our lover will be wearing tonight.

The more we use the seer in a lighthearted way, to make predictions for ordinary, zany, everyday moments, the more in tune we'll be when we really need it, when an accurate prediction means the difference between life and death.

Go ahead and make ten fun predictions today, from what color hair your waitress will have, to how many bills are in the mailbox. Don't be afraid of mistakes. Go wild. Be a psychic nut-cake.

SEVEN MORE WAYS TO ACTIVATE THE SEER

1. Give yourself or a friend a reading based solely on what you see in the eyes—their color, shape, emotional expression, depth. If you don't know the person, write the information in your notebook as a free verse eye poem. Some cultures say that the left eye is the spirit eye and the right eye is the human eye. Do you agree? Test this hypothesis. Study your eyes together and separately.

2. Read writers who use a lot of rich imagery. When you come to a word-picture that drives you senses wild, close your eyes and stay in the picture until it fills your whole body. Pablo Neruda, e.e. cummings, Michael Ondaatje, Anaïs Nin, Margaret Atwood, Tom Robbins, Richard Brautigan, and Robert Bly are some examples of writers who have a paintbrush at the end of their pen.

3. Sit on a chair and meditate with your eyes open in front of a full-length mirror for ten minutes a day. Try turning off the lights and lighting some candles. From ages fourteen to twenty, this was my favorite meditation technique. It taught me how to see colors and track energy currents. Be patient with this exercise. It might take several tries before your eyes remember how to see your soul.

4. Watch foreign films that have lots of dreamscapes, many moving images and symbols, and minimal dialogue, from Ingmar

Bergman to Akira Kurosawa. Both of these fellows are master seers. There are no boundaries, no limits to what enters their camera.

5. Become an observer of details: nail polish color, insects, dust, lost pennies, how people hold their coffee mug, birds, breezes, smiles. This will sharpen your awareness, and give you a more intuitive, poetic perspective of life.

6. Do some spontaneous painting, where you let go of form and structure and allow the images and colors that are moving through you to appear on paper. This will help you unfreeze visionary blocks, and give the seer a chance to speak without words. If you think you have no painting talent, read *Paint, Life, and Passion* by Michell Cassou and Stewart Cubley. It started me painting, and I am about as skilled with a paintbrush as Curious George.

7. Give yourself lots of time to daydream. Before falling asleep at night, take a mind trip to anywhere in the universe you want, real or imaginary; or pretend you are a satellite floating in space, staring back at the earth with cosmic ease. Daydreams are like yoga stretches for the seer, warm-ups, practice for a brave, visionary life.

PART III

Awakening the Empath

Feelings

I feel, therefore I am.

 Feelings are the subtlest form of communication humans share. They are more discreet than words; feelings bypass the intellect and slip into the bloodstream, the bones, the cells. Feelings are the music of the body, the melodies that float through the nervous system and ignite the heart. Of all the landscapes we travel through, feeling is the most terrifying. There are no boundaries; the depths are unexpected and grueling, and the heights force us to change our lives.

Growing up, many of us were taught that feelings were irrational, that real insight arrives through the mind, through reason and philosophical inquiry. As a psychic, I've learned the opposite. I've come to trust my feelings more than anything else. Visions can sometimes be off, thoughts can come out lopsided, but feelings never lie. When I am in tune with my feelings, my readings are clear as water. The only time a feeling becomes inaccurate is when it is overanalyzed, dissected, given false words. Otherwise they are the most reliable source of guidance we have.

In order for your feelings to become psychic and lead you on your soul's path, you have to be intimate with them, willing to explore the full range of sensations that pass through your body. Modern society is not geared toward this style of living. Everything we do is about escape, about running away from our feelings into a realm of pleasure and distraction. Speed is becoming a world trend. I gave a session to some students from Hong Kong who told me that back home city life moves even faster than it does here. In the huge corporations, people eat lunch in about five minutes. Elevators climb buildings like rocketships. Pedestrians overtake joggers.

Awakening the empath requires that we slow down, breathe, absorb our feelings in a more primitive rhythm. When we are rushing, the empath falls behind and our intuition diminishes. We might receive a message, a picture, or a sound, but if our heart is absent, we won't know what it means.

Some feelings our soul sends us are as fine as silk, a nudging, a caress, a whisper. Others tear into us with the intensity of Beethoven, pushing us in a new direction like a wave crashing against a boat. When you allow all these movements to inhabit your body, without any mental interference, you start to feel the presence of your soul in everything you do. As the Persian poet Rumi said, "Beauty surrounds us, but usually we need to be walking in a garden to know it." When you're at one with your feelings, you don't need any evidence that your soul exists. You can sense it inside you, pulsing through your cells. You are no longer indebted to others for guidance—your body becomes your psychic.

Carl Jung, the Swiss psychologist, considered feeling a rational function, "one of the ways in which our consciousness obtains its orientation to experience." It is with feeling that we decide who we can trust, what our passions are, what foods work well in our body. When we block out our feelings, we are in a sense making ourselves lost, tearing the pin from our compass and still expecting to find our way home.

In the next part of this chapter, I will give you a list of rituals you can perform to clear a pathway so your real feelings may speak to you and make you more psychic. All of us have contrived internal barriers that get in the way of our soul being fully expressed in our body. These rituals will help you dissolve your armor, the numbness that stands between you and the empath. This is not easy work. Opening ourselves to feeling requires a great deal of courage, patience, and trust. It's like swimming in the ocean. You never know what current is going to touch you next.

◎ Journal Writing

Journal writing is one of the best ways to develop intimacy with your feelings, to expose the voice of your soul in its most naked form. Without this dialogue, we never fully understand who we are. As songwriter Leonard Cohen said, "Men steadfastly refuse to eavesdrop on themselves." This is true for most humans. It is scary to be an observer of ourselves, to examine our character without the distance of rational thoughts.

The purpose of journal writing is to lose control, to dig into yourself like a lover and let your innermost secrets be revealed: poems, fantasies, dreams, stories. Journal writing is not only about self-evaluation. It's about getting the blood moving, stepping into a world where there is no shame, embarrassment, fear, criticism. It is in this landscape that the soul feels comfortable to express itself. When we are emotionally uninhibited, it is easy to be psychic. We can talk to ourselves without restraint, let the messages that our conscious mind has been resisting come rushing through our pen.

A journal should be safe only in the sense that it is private. Otherwise it should be a total risk, a place where you can be naked, without reserve, stripped to the core. When I write in my journal, I don't even like to punctuate. I prefer the madness of run-on sentences. I let my arm rip across the page like a lawnmower. If I want to scream, I scream. I make it a full body experience. I write blindly, surprised by each word that comes out of me. Some of the best psychic readings I have received have been in my journal. If I want a question answered, I just ask it. Then I write the response. You can't stop to think if you want your journal to be an instinctual experience. It will ruin the flow. You have to keep your pen moving.

Natalie Goldberg's book *Writing Down the Bones* taught me a great deal about how to write in a journal. She is a student of Zen, a believer in the old saying, "First thought, best thought." Read her books if you have trouble writing without your head. Also, read the upcoming chapter called "Language." It will teach you more ways to be psychic with your pen.

Each set of feelings we carry has a different voice, a unique persona. In your journal, let all your personalities speak: the skeptic, the dreamer, the realist, the lover, the artist. If one voice is dominating, find its counterbalance. I have a voice inside me whom I named Margaret. She's a drag queen, a witty cross-dresser who absolutely loves to give dangerous advice. She balances out my diplomatic side. She's brave and fiery, always advising me to be honest, to not sugarcoat my words, to be a writer who tickles people with truth.

If you don't hold back, journal writing can be a riveting experience, a way to map out your inner theater, and expose new voices, instincts, passions. It will teach you how to become intimate with yourself, aware of the many intuitive feelings that speak to you throughout the day. Read famous journals to inspire you if you get stuck. Anaïs Nin's work changed my life. My readings greatly improved after studying her books, and traveling with her through the many corridors of the heart.

◎ Breathing

Breath and feeling are interconnected. When we are nervous, our breath speeds up; when we are relaxed, it slows down, sinks into the belly. The nature and rhythm of our breath affects how we perceive the world. When we change our breath, we change our awareness, our brain chemistry, how we see life. Yogis have known this for thousands of years. They use breath to transform themselves, to descend into a near-death sleep, or vault into the electrical rapture of the gods.

In the realm of psychic development, conscious breathing helps you detect vibrations in your nervous system, the subtle messages transmitted from your soul to your physical body. A lot of the intuitive cues we receive are very quiet. To interpret them we need to have calm breath flowing through us, stable lungs filling us with air.

During a reading, whenever I get lost and out of touch with the material, I always turn to my breath for support. This centers me, allowing more room for intuitive sensations to pass through my body. Trying to be psychic when your breath is fast and out of control is like trying to read poetry while jogging. You have to be still inside to catch all the nuances, the small blips on your screen.

Our breath is like a vacuum. It draws in data not only from the soul, but also from other people and the exact ideas, perceptions, and feelings we need to nourish our being. I have experienced this with my wife when we meditate together; we are feeding off each other, sharing energetic nutrients through pathways of breath.

Whenever you want to be more intuitive in a situation—to know how your lover is feeling, why your child is angry, when you should speak in a conversation—just breathe more. Take relaxed inhalations and monitor all the information that passes through you. In each moment of life there is a different rhythm, a shifting group energy. When you pay attention to your breath, you start to feel what this rhythm is. Your cells open up to the subtle frequencies of space. Like a jazz musician, you begin to sense what instrument is going to be played next, what key you are in, when the music is going to end.

When you are breathing well, it is impossible to suppress your feelings. You leave a place of guessing and enter a place of knowing. It puts you in a state of sharp awareness. Whatever psychic sensations you need to receive become more apparent. Your sensors get clearer. What is subtle with scattered breath becomes obvious with calm breath.

Breath is the primary ingredient of alertness. When we breathe well, our consciousness is refined. We enter the realm of cats and trees and spiders. The beautiful thing about breath is that not only does it enhance our intuition, it also protects us, creates a healthy boundary that edits harmful energies. When we breathe well, our body finds its balance, the clarity we need to hear the empath.

◎ Meditation

A lot of people use meditation to escape feelings, to raise themselves to a higher level of consciousness, a seat in the clouds where human pain can't touch them. This is a necessary practice to attain the broad vision of the shaman, but in order for meditation to link you with your intuition, you need to stay on the ground, to travel into your feelings rather than away from them.

You don't need any mantras, prayers, visualizations, invocations. These might be helpful in other psychic realms, but with the empath you need to be in a state of listening, of pure receptivity, with no barriers between you and your emotions.

The heart has a different voice from the mind. To hear it, we must go inward, pay attention to each feeling we have and track it to the source. Until we really explore a feeling, we often judge it, giving it a label that denigrates its value. Feelings are like rivers. They transport valuable materials: messages, ideas, guidance. If we push down a feeling without examining it, we are sabotaging ourselves, throwing away a precious gift.

Many feelings when they first enter us have an uncomfortable texture, like the skin of a fruit, bitter and rough. But if we hold on and venture inward, there is always a sweetness of psychic food. At the core of our stress or anger might be a creative idea that wants to burst forth, a poem, a prediction, or some healing advice. Deep sadness might carry in it the song of release and transformation. You never know what a feeling is carrying until you experience it, until you get still and meditative enough that it enters your blood.

The feelings that we absolutely must explore are the ones that send off an alarm in our body, that make us want to scream, sob, or push us into a state of detachment or paralysis. In these moments it is crucial that we meditate and let the feeling have its full expression in our body. This doesn't mean that you need to start yelling or sobbing. Feelings can be experienced without a dramatic release. You can have a full temper tantrum without uttering a word, by just closing your eyes and turning into fire.

The feelings that give us the most hardship, that keep returning again and again, triggered by a myriad of experiences, are usually connected to old wounds we haven't healed yet: the death of a parent, an abusive marriage, a high school heartbreak. When you meditate on these feelings, you will be taken on a psychic journey back to the source of the pain. The empath will guide you into the past and show you where you need to heal yourself, so that you may complete the circle and move forward as a whole human being.

I have found it best to perform this style of meditation at uncomfortable moments of the day, when your body is charged with stress, exhaustion, anger, or anxiety. The moment you feel an overload, go somewhere and sit for five or ten minutes, cross-legged or in a chair, whatever you like better. Once you are seated, close your eyes and just let your feelings run through you. Don't try to stop them. Let them sink into you like knives, fire, rain, hail.

Surrender your defenses and breathe in a rhythm that matches the feeling. If you are stressed or angry, start your breath a little faster, and then bring it to an even flow, a speed that allows you to stay listening to all the feelings in your body.

Meditating in this manner a few times a day will bring you into closer range with your feelings and teach you how to absorb into your consciousness the intuitive messages each feeling carries. It will also make you a better people reader. There will be less reaction time when you meet someone. You will know right away what you feel, and how you should act.

The only reason we enter spaces of vagueness, uncertainty, or inner confusion is that we are disconnected from our feelings. When we bridge the gap, erasing the line between our head and our heart, we can know the world intimately right away, enter into the depths of another person and sense their motives in the flash of an eye.

Having this kind of speed with our feelings can save us a lot of grief, protecting us from harmful relationships, indigestion, illness. In becoming our own psychic, this immediacy with our true feelings is an absolute must.

In Part V, "Invoking the Shaman," I will show you a meditation technique that activates some of the more luminous psychic senses, enabling you to talk with guides and spirits. For the empath, there is nothing you need to do but sit, breathe, and feel. This is it.

Before I got married, my feelings were cut in half. People thought I was the calmest person in the world, because I had become a master of numbing my pain. My psychic readings were accurate, but they lacked the truth of the heart, the empathy needed to reveal a person's deepest sorrow and lead them to healing.

When I met Raïna, my friend, wife, and teacher, all of this changed. With her soulful fire, she woke me up, guided me in a million directions of healing. After being with her for three years, I gained an intimacy with my body I had not experienced since childhood. I went to therapy, movement classes, writing workshops. I studied meditation, martial arts, weight lifting. Raïna got me hooked on feeling. I learned to live as Bagwhan Rajneesh suggested to his disciples: "Mad from the heart."

The rituals I showed you are a starting point. If you really want to ignite your intuition, to be in rapport with the world through your feelings, you might need to try as many routes as I have, brave roads of physical and emotional healing, so that the voice of the empath may be heard in your body.

By starting this journey, you will be drawn to all the right people, the right classes, the right books. Remember, let your heart tell you who is worthy of being your teacher. People who are not open to their feelings, to being vulnerable and human, are not worth studying with. You will gather more information, more lists, but you won't grow.

Listening

Listening is a form of accepting.
—STELLA TERRIL MANN

 In many myths, the psychic lives in darkness, and his insights arise from a deep listening rather than from the colors and shapes of the outside world. And many stories include the character of the wise blind man, who has no physical vision but is able to read people with extraordinary clarity. This kind of intuitive sensing begins in the ears. Through the pathway of hearing, we learn how to interpret the world on the most intimate level, gathering psychic information into the depths of our being.

As children, our hearing was much more developed. When we listened to a song or the rain on the roof, we took it in with our whole bodies. There was an ecstasy in hearing. We craved new sounds—a siren, a horn, a squeak from a toy. By the time we are adults, many of us lose this excitement. We start to listen less consciously, as a backdrop to other activities. We don't have time anymore to let a whole Jimi Hendrix album crank through our bodies, or sit in the park and savor the wind for a while. Even a lot of musicians and therapists I know use music as just a backdrop, never really going into sound, into pure listening. It is no wonder that so many of us in our old age suffer from hearing disorders.

It's a habit in our culture to tune life out, until eventually you hear nothing at all.

Just as you lose your sense of balance when your ears are plugged, so does your empathic ability decrease when you stop really listening to the world. There is a deep link between psychic receptivity and everyday hearing. When one weakens, so does the other. In order for us to hear the subtle messages of the soul, we need to have our ears tuned to life, to the many levels of sound and vibration that pass through our space. The arts and entertainment of the twentieth century are centered on vision, the eyes, the surface of things. To become psychic, you need to reverse this trend, to pay homage to listening in all its forms.

◎ Music

I remember British philosopher Alan Watts saying in a lecture that music is the most spiritual of the arts because it is the most ephemeral. He said in the West we see sacredness in things that appear permanent, eternal, everlasting, like a mountain or a sea, but in the East, holiness is attributed to that which is fleeting, transitory, out of reach. Music has these qualities. It flies through the senses and then disappears, like a phantom, leaving nothing but a memory, a wave of feelings to prove its existence.

For this reason, music is an excellent teacher for refining psychic awareness. The intuitive messages our body sends us have the same elusive nature as the notes in a song; they are transient, mysterious, hard to catch. When we learn to listen to music more attentively, as a meditation, the signals inside us become more tangible. We learn to hear the empath the moment she is speaking, with less interference from our rational mind.

In his tape *The New Physics of Healing,* Deepak Chopra says that when information enters our body from the quantum field, it is smaller than thought. We usually don't sense it in our consciousness until it has snowballed into something bigger: an idea, a concept, a fear. Listening to music enhances our receptivity. We become alert and open enough to seize an impulse in its pure form, and follow it through in perfect harmony with our soul. This kind of timing is what makes an event feel like a miracle. When there is no space between your actions and your instincts, whatever you are doing becomes luminous.

There are many different types of music you can use to arouse your psychic senses. There is a giant wave of New Age music flooding the marketplace right now, but a lot of it takes you out of your emotions into a realm of white light and angelic tranquility. To connect with the empath, you need music that draws you down into the bones, the blood, the emotional centers of the body. To invoke the shaman, New Age music is wonderful, but for the empath, you need music that is human, songs that take you onto the traveling road of the heart. Some suggestions: Beethoven, Mozart, Geoffrey Okema, Joni Mitchell, Peter Gabriel (especially the soundtrack for *The Last Temptation of Christ*), Leonard Cohen, Annie Lennox (especially *Diva*), Wagner.

If you don't have any music like this in your home, do some research. Go into record stores and sample albums until you find something that really touches you, makes your eyes water. This could be a fun psychic exercise . . . music shopping with your sixth sense!

Once you've found something you like, go home, lie down on the floor or on the couch, and devote yourself to a good forty-five minutes of deep listening. If you have some headphones, put them on. You also might want to close the blinds and light a candle. Creating a ritual atmosphere will make it easier to become intimate with the music, enter a sound vacuum where the empath can speak to you.

As you are listening, imagine tiny sensors all over your skin receiving the music. Feel the music not just as sounds, but also as a frequency, an intricate code channeling through your body. Occasionally follow one instrument as it travels on its course. Then let everything melt together again, like raindrops splashing into a puddle. Music can be experienced as a series of auditory details or a wave of vibrant energy. Go back and forth. See how many different perspectives you can achieve in a single song.

Whatever emotions grab you, whatever subtle or wild sensations twist through your heart, let them have their full expression. Don't suppress anything. Let your body follow its own instinctual pathways.

After ten or fifteen minutes of listening, imagine the music as a liquid pouring into your heart, a green river healing painful emotions and feelings. Visualize a circle of heat where the sound can enter. Place both of your hands on your chest. This is the home of the empath. Get used to the sudden insights that arise from this area of the body.

When the music is over, stay on your back for five minutes and rest in the space you have carved out. Stay listening. What is your body saying to you? Do you want to cry, sing, scream, dance? Doing this exercise will give you a greater understanding of what your body is craving, what emotions or activities you need to integrate into your life to stay growing. Make a mental list of everything the music has inspired you to do. Then, when you have some time, begin incorporating these elements into your daily life.

Before you get up, do a little stretching. Come back to consciousness in a slow, methodical manner. If you want, write down in your journal some of the different feelings that passed through your body as you were taking in the music. This will strengthen your intuition, and give you a reference point for how it feels to be fully engaged in psychic listening.

Try this exercise with both instrumental and vocal music, and see which one gives you better results, which style provides you with a more immediate connection to your body.

You can do this exercise before a date, an interview, or a meeting with a friend. Even five minutes of focused listening while you are at home or waiting in the car will place you in a more intuitive, receptive state of being.

Final note. Pay attention to the songs you hear on the radio, in shopping malls, doctors' offices. Lots of time a lyric or a melody can have synchronistic value, giving you a message to help you cope with your day, or simply reminding you that you are not alone, that all the chaos of the world has a meaningful order.

◎ Poetry

Reading and listening to poetry has long been a method of awakening the heart. Poets are often spoken of as having great depth of feeling, as individuals who are in tune with the nuances of life, subtle layers of beauty that most of us overlook.

In modern culture, poetry has taken a backseat to other more popular writing genres. It seems that many of us don't have the time or patience for poetry anymore. We want to read things that are more practical, that have a specific purpose: the newspaper, magazines, self-help books. The problem is, these genres of writing don't provide us with the same sensory refinement that poetry does. They inform us of certain technical information, but unlike poetry, they do not awaken in us the music of the body, the graceful frequencies through which the empath communicates.

I started reading poetry when I was thirteen. It was a perfect prelude to being a psychic. With poetry, I learned how to listen, how to derive from words secret intuitive meanings. Poetry drew me into the core of myself, the place where language and the body meet.

How we read or listen to poetry determines how it affects us, to what degree it enhances our intuitive pathways. I read a fantastic book on haiku called *The Seeds of Birch*, wherein the author taught the reader a precise method for reading these little Japanese poems. He said that a haiku must first be memorized, spoken out loud until you are able to recite it without looking at the page. Then you must repeat the haiku slowly in your head, and at the same time, watch the images of the poem as they move inside you, in slow motion . . . hearing them, feeling them, breathing them . . . only then will you get the real meaning the haiku carries.

To develop the empath, you must read poetry with the same inward attention. You must enter the landscape of the poem, feel each word as it slips into your body. Worry about understanding the poem later on. In the beginning, just read and feel, savoring each phrase as you would a cloud in the sky or a strawberry in your mouth. A poem is a sensual experience. Just because it has words doesn't mean you have to define it. Just give it to the empath. Let your intuition inform you what jewel the poem is carrying. A poem is a vehicle of feelings more than thoughts. When you read poetry, your heart is the interpreter.

Rilke, one of my favorite poets, wrote a book called *Sonnets to Orpheus*, which has in it many references to inner listening. Pablo Neruda is also a great poet to read to develop the inner ear. His poems have a rhythm and sensuality that reach far into the body, into the primal depths from which our intuition rises.

The poets that will not help you awaken the empath are the academic poets, such as Wallace Stevens and Ezra Pound, whose verse is cerebral and intellectually dense. Their poems are brain teasers, but not inspiring to the heart. In poetry, simplicity and clarity are vital to awakening your inner hearing. The soul is easily muted by the din of complex language.

Lately, the poet that has been an important teacher for me, a real psychic guide, is Rumi, the Persian mystic. He is a poet of the hundred senses, able to travel through space without leaving the ground. Reading his work has increased my ability to feel, to sense the world through instinct and vision. *The Complete Works of Rumi*, translated by Coleman Barks, is a superb collection of his writing.

If reading poetry on your own is not that exciting, invite one of your friends over and take turns reading to each other. As the listener, lie down on your back as you did with the music, and feel the words and images sink into your skin, from your toes to your hair. Make love to the sounds, the hidden meanings, the spaces of mystery.

See if you can feel in your body what the writer is like in real life, how words pass through his consciousness, what his motives are, what he was like as a child. Often it is the feeling behind the words that moves us—the writer's heart, and not his diction, that feeds our soul.

After hearing a few poems, read some for your friend. Escort each other back and forth into the world of sound. If your lover enjoys poetry, by all means do the ritual together. The more intimate you are with a person, the more the poetry will come to life and awaken your inner hearing. In my house, poetry is our prayer. My wife and I use it to communicate with each other, to share intuitive messages from heart to heart.

My best readings are like poems, the way the words come out of me, the nuances, the magic. When I am at my best, I am not a psychic. I am a poet.

◉ Listening to the World

There are many opportunities we have during the day to train our listening: while we are walking down the street, shopping, sitting in traffic, roaming through the park. We can refine our hearing anywhere, by opening ourselves up to subtle vibrations of sound at all moments of the day.

One night I was sitting in the restaurant where I give readings, feeling a little overwhelmed by the noise of the people streaming to tables, cracking jokes, yelling. I decided to open my body to the deeper sounds of the room. I started breathing in calm intervals and surrendered to the intense noise of the restaurant. At first nothing happened. I kept breathing slowly, imagining my hearing encompassing my entire body. I visualized my knees listening, my arms, my feet. I made myself into a chamber of sound, a miniature auditorium.

Out of the blue, the annoyance of the sound disappeared. Through my breath and focused listening, I had changed my aware- ness. The sounds were now exhilarating. The restaurant was still loud—a circus of frying pans and clashing voices—but now I was inside the sound. I was no longer a victim of it. I could enjoy the chaos, could receive the aggressive noise without any stress on my body.

After a few minutes of listening like this, I was in ecstasy. I had reached the frequency in the room where the sound was harmoni- ous and unabrasive. Not only was my hearing more refined, but my psychic ability had also increased. When I watched people, I was able to sense exactly what they were feeling, what type of thoughts were circulating through their head. The listening exercise had taken me deeply not only into my own being, but also into the bodies of other people. I was reading the room from the inside out, no longer a stranger to those around me.

Just as some feelings have a rough outer layer that must be broken through to get to the sweetness, many sounds also require a meditative state of awareness to be appreciated. Especially in the modern world, a lot of the sounds we hear each day are not familiar to our bodies. Our hearing has not evolved to assimilate comfort- ably the many industrial frequencies that bombard us as we move through the city. We have to become our own sound harmonizer, bringing the dissonance of the world into our own physical balance.

I am not suggesting that you practice listening to car alarms and microwave buzzers, but if you are in a situation where you are being accosted by intense sound, remember that you have a choice as to how you receive it. The only way to feel relaxed in certain circumstances is to become the sound—to surrender and be taken over by the chaotic waves of energy. This exercise will work well for you if you are very sensitive, someone whose nerves are close to the skin.

At the other end of the scale, it is also important for empathic development to practice hearing subtle sounds, going into nature and tuning into the discreet hush of moving leaves, chirping cicadas, trickling streams. The subtle frequencies of nature, when listened to with the sensors of the body, will help awaken your instinctual senses. Native Americans practice this all the time. They hear the wind speaking to them, receive messages from crickets and frogs. In Herman Hesse's book *Siddhartha,* the main character achieves enlightenment by listening to the river, by yielding his mind to the wisdom of flowing water. The same meditation I performed in the restaurant will work in the forest. The important thing is to envision your whole body hearing, all your cells receiving sound.

The more you refine your hearing, the more connected you will feel to the world around you. There are many times that a car horn or a bird call has given me a specific insight, notifying me of a synchronicity that was about to occur, or flashing me a warning to wake up and be alert. When you let sounds sink into you and touch your intuitive field of awareness, the whole world becomes your guide.

The empath is always listening, translating sounds into meaning, noises into messages and insights. This process is mysterious and deeply personal. How you hear the world is as unique as how you feel or see it. Above all, trust your own methods, your own style of psychic listening.

◉ Conversation

Listening is the most important element in a conversation. Speaking is secondary. When you are listening well, much can be understood through silence, through the space between words. When one or both people are not listening, it is impossible to have an intuitive dialogue. The telepathic circuits are blocked. A lot of talk goes down, but each person remains in a separate world.

In conversation, a great way to enhance your empathic ability is to take the most meaningful sentences a person is speaking and repeat them slowly in your head. This will force the words to fall deeper, to penetrate the chaos of your thinking and awaken a sharper intimacy.

Also, pay attention to the voice. As we are speaking, many different voices come out of us. One moment we will be speaking from the adult part of ourselves—rational, focused, precise—and the next second the voice of the child will bubble up. Our speaking tone will rise a few notes and our bodies will feel open and vulnerable. I noticed these vocal transitions when I heard the Dalai Lama speak. His voice had many personalities, from the somber mystic to the ecstatic four-year-old. When we listen to a voice separate from the words, as a kind of music, it reveals a lot about a person. It helps us understand how he feels in his body, what his childhood was like, whether or not he was listened to growing up or locked in a tomb of silence.

Being focused in a conversation can also help us identify if someone is lying or telling the truth. When someone is speaking honestly, from the heart, there is an increase in energy that warms the room and dissolves physical space. When someone is hiding something, or communicating only part of the story, your body will pick up a restrictive feeling. The voice becomes flat, like the lid of a pot covering a mysterious sauce.

During conversation, you can also tune in to the body of the person who is speaking, observing her gestures and mannerisms. When we talk, we say a lot more than what comes out of our mouth. Our whole body projects ideas, thoughts, energies, sensations. That which slips through our voice box is only part of our expression. The majority of our communication is silent, a series of subtle feelings and emotions that emanate from the skin.

Speaking is one of the most difficult things we do each day. Even those people who blabber away at nine hundred miles an hour experience the anxiety of verbal communication. Keeping your breath calm and steady when you speak, and allowing yourself time to pause and digest your feelings, will allow your intuition to mingle with your words.

Paradoxically, it is also important in conversation to sometimes rush ahead without thinking. I do this all the time in my readings. When there is an opening, a moment of divine magic, I will leap into flights of poetry, let new sentence structures and word-pictures influence my ideas, speed up, slow down, shift intonations, shout, whisper. This, too, is part of listening—being in tune with where the words are coming from and carrying them into the air with the appropriate intensity.

When we are unaware of our speech, we develop rigid patterns of communication that stifle our psychic voice. If you wish to express the empath, you can't hold on to only one vocal style. The soul is diverse and shifting. You need to adapt, to draw words from all corners of your being, allow a multitude of tones to inhabit your body.

In conversation, listening to your inner being is just as vital as listening to the other person. When you do this, a higher power emerges. The conversation widens. Creative ideas become more available. Psychic information pours through you. The ear and tongue form a golden partnership.

I am an Aries. For me, listening has always been a challenge. My head is usually swirling with so many thoughts and ideas that to hear what another person is saying often requires a lot of effort. I have to bolt my mouth closed, sit still in my chair, and breathe deeply.

It is only recently that I have discovered how blissful it is to be present while another person is communicating. I never realized until I started doing readings how starved most of us are for attention, how rare it is in modern society that people are patient and open enough to hear our story.

Now listening is a sacred activity. Whether it be the siren of a firetruck, the wind, the laughter of a child—these are all voices, sounds from the Great Creator to guide us through the day.

Voices

When a voice has heart it can heal a million people.
—Dr. Hubert

 We all hear voices in our heads. You don't have to live in a padded cell to subscribe to the talking channel. There is something about the human brain that enjoys being in dialogue with itself, to separate into many characters and engage in conversation. The challenge we have in developing our psychic ability is to weed out from this forum of chatter the real voice, the intuitive voice, the voice that has the insight to direct us on our soul's path.

As I have learned from my readings, most of us follow the voices we internalized growing up. Rather than being guided by our soul, we are pushed through life by the voice of our mother, our father, the media, our friends. The psyche is porous. It is easy for us to absorb a voice from the outside world and let it control our lives.

I have experienced this with a lot of my clients. Someone will ask me a question about what law school they should go to, or whether or not they should marry a certain person, and rather than hearing their voice ask the question, intuitively I will hear the voice of their parents or society. When I tell them that, there is usually a great sigh of relief. It's like removing a dust cover from a beautiful vase. Now they can choose. They no longer have to enroll themselves in someone else's future. They can follow their own voice, go where it is their heart is calling.

A lot of our insecurities, doubts, fears, and anxieties are voices we have picked up from other people, old tapes that get in the way of our own music. "You're fat. You're not an artist. You'll never get married." When you engage the voice of your soul, your intuitive guide, these false voices start to fade away. The mind gets more and more quiet, until eventually, the only one left speaking is you.

◎ The Voice That Heals

The first thing to know about your inner voice is that it heals. No matter what it sounds like, whether it is has a religious tone or is sharp and scientific, the voice is a messenger of love. It will not tear you apart with insults, threats, paranoia. When you are in league with this voice, you are spoken to with calmness, certainty, and smooth understanding.

My inner voice has the qualities of an old man, someone who conveys valuable information in simple words. He says things like "Slow down" when I am driving too fast, or "Talk to the woman in the blue suit" when I am at a party. He leads the way by walking behind me, by filling my sails with perfect measurements of wind.

The first step in getting in touch with your inner voice is to imagine how it would feel to be spoken to by someone who has real wisdom, how this voice would reverberate in your body when it gave you advice. Maybe you heard such a person speak on the radio one time? Maybe an actor you admire has a voice like this, or a singer or poet.

Once you have a general idea of how this voice would sound, enter into meditation and hear it speaking through your being. The moment you awaken the possibility of having a wise voice— a psychic guide—inside you, the voice will appear. As children, we were always talking with ourselves, always conversing with our soul. This kind of dialogue was natural to us.

Invite the voice to speak to you and trust the process. The moment you get a response, a nibble on your line, ask the voice questions, talk with it, and inform it that you would like its guidance in your daily life. Think of the voice as your oracle, a psychic you can turn to when you're lost on the path. If a picture comes to you of the voice as you are speaking to it, file it in your memory. A visual impression will make the dialogue more real. Your inner voice might not even look human. It might just be a bright light or an ancient symbol. Trust what you see.

After a while, you and the voice will merge. The voice will start to speak to you without your turning it on. It will become a part of your awareness, visit you in difficult situations, tell you what street to turn down to avoid an accident, what book to buy, whom you should call that day who needs your love.

Having an inner voice is not strange or far-out. Once you get in the habit of listening to it, it will become an ordinary part of your life. Instead of your hearing shouts of fear and anxiety in your head, the host of your talk show will be calm, someone you can rely on in shaky moments.

If you become very in sync with your inner voice, a lot of the time you won't even hear it in words. The dialogue will be extremely subtle. A wave of feeling will pass through you and you'll know what the voice is saying. A meditation teacher I know says, "If something you do makes you feel more open, then it is good for you. If something closes you down, then it is bad." Our inner voice communicates with the same simplicity. It is our brain that complicates things. The soul is clear and direct.

Final note: If a moment comes when you really need this voice but cannot hear it above your own mental chatter, take ten slow breaths and relax your body. The noise of the mind quickly vanishes when our body is carrying smooth breath. Confusion thrives on jumpy nerves and frayed circuits. Just breathe slowly and the voice will return.

Take some time each day to listen to your inner voice. In the morning and night, sit in a quiet place and ask yourself three questions that you would ask a psychic or psychologist concerning things you should do in your future. Start with small questions and work your way up. What restaurant should I go to for dinner? How is my mother feeling today? Whom should I write a letter to?

Write down the exact answers the voice tells you. If the answers resonate with your heart, if they make you feel good inside, follow them and see what happens. At some point in our life, we have to take the reins in our own hands. This is a good way to start.

◉ Projecting Your Inner Voice

There are many times in the day when we want to tell somebody something and realize the air is too dense for words. The comment "You look beautiful" or "I love you" might be too cumbersome for the room, distract the flow of conversation, and make the other person embarrassed or self-conscious.

In these moments you can project your psychic voice from your mind rather than speaking it. As Gary Zukav discusses in his book *Seat of the Soul,* we are multidimensional beings. It is natural for us to communicate with each other in many frequencies at once. The voice in us that comes from our soul often wants to say something sweet and caring that as humans will make us feel awkward. Speaking through the mind, in wavelengths of silent feeling, can be an effective way to communicate affection to strangers and the people we love when the moment is too fragile for words.

During the day, we are constantly bombarded by trivial events, which make us frazzled, annoyed, or angry. When you see someone in one of these irritated states, you can project to them a soothing message: "Relax, everything is okay, slow down . . ." Doing this can be tremendously healing, help someone regain their balance before they drift out of control.

The soul is constantly wanting to express love. As humans, we are often afraid of transmitting this through the spoken word. Rather than judging ourselves for this fear, we can let our love be expressed in silence, in streams of mindful feeling. The more you do this, the easier it will be to express affection with words, to carry deep emotions through your voice. Projecting words from the mind is a way of training yourself for verbal intimacy. All powers originate inside us. The best poetry begins in silence.

As you are intuitively sending words, you will notice people brightening up around you; they may sigh, or breathe deeply, or for no reason at all, break into a wide smile. The empath is connected to a frequency of healing, an invisible dialogue between the bodies of all living things. When you begin to participate in this reality, you will start to feel safer, more at ease. You will begin to emanate a warmth that people trust, and become a magnet for meaningful relationships.

To make this process more powerful, as you are projecting the words, visualize a rush of energy pouring from the center of your chest into the person's heart. This will expand your magnetic field

Dreams

When man is dreaming he is a genius.
—AKIRA KUROSAWA

 It is only in the past hundred years or so that humans have used dreams as a vehicle for psychological evaluation. Before people like Freud and Jung came along, dreams had more to do with prophecy than with self-discovery. When someone in a village had a dream, he interpreted it as an event that was going to happen in his waking life: a flood, a new baby, an attack from a neighboring tribe. Through the symbols and images they received while sleeping, people derived literal meanings, much the same way a seer does with Tarot cards or Rune stones. Dreams were like news reports from the stars. What you saw at night had a direct relation to the day.

Since we have stopped viewing our dreams in this manner, as harbingers of future events, our dreaming style has changed. As the Heidegger Principle goes, the observer affects what is being observed. Now that we see our dreams as reflections of our psychological condition, for the most part, that is how they come to us. Our dreams are no longer as psychic as they used to be, because we have altered their nature, stopped believing in them as prophetic visions and more as metaphorical stories. This was an important step in our evolution. We needed to stop taking the cosmos so and broaden your range of psychic perception, so that you can actually feel the body of another person without physically touching them.

Try using your inner voice with plants and animals as well. They know this level of sound. They share it with each other all the time.

Since I have been in contact with my inner voice, my life is a lot smoother. A lot of the worry and fear I inherited from my childhood has been replaced by calmness. The voice I have found knows things are eternal—that if I miss this bus, there is another one coming. When you start to hear your inner voice, you'll realize how ancient you are, how much stardust is in your suitcase. At a moment you would otherwise be consumed with panic, you will be winking inside.

literally. It was driving us mad. A dream of a black horse could mean the end of the world was coming. Superstitions were getting the better of us. The town streets were full of Chicken Littles.

Now as we approach the year 2000, the pendulum is swinging back in the other direction. With all the rapid changes in the world, and the increased need for self-guidance, there is once again a demand for psychic dreams, ways in which the soul can inspire our daily choices. We are moving into a time of survival, where taking the right plane, selecting the right doctor, or drinking the right glass of water could have an impact on our lives.

In the next part of this chapter, I will show you various ways you can influence your dreams to become more psychic, so that the empath can speak with you and escort you through the day. By no means am I saying that you should start taking your dreams literally right away. There is no need to jump back to a state of medieval paranoia and declare every bad dream as an omen of the plague. Developing psychic sleep states needs to be done gradually, with a lot of common sense and inner listening. Follow the exercises and trust your instincts.

◎ Remembering Your Dreams

As humans, we never stop dreaming. It is part of our biology, something common to all mammals. These nocturnal stories go on inside us whether we remember them or not. It is only in the denial of our soul, our creativity, our passion, that our dream line is severed and we wake up each morning with a blank mind.

If this is the case for you, before moving on to the next part of the chapter, do one or more of the following exercises to reignite your dream memory. They are simple and direct. Even the desire to remember your dreams can bring them back into your life.

Before you fall asleep at night, whisper this sentence to yourself three times: "When I awake, I will remember all my dreams. When I awake, I will remember all my dreams . . ." Feel the desire in your heart as you are saying it. Feel your whole body opening to your dreams.

* * *

Select a dream image from your past that left a deep impression on you and paint a picture of it in any style you wish: abstract, realist, cubist. When it is finished, hang it on the wall in your bedroom. Drawing the portrait will help you remember your dreams on a more regular basis. The artist and the dreamer are connected. When one is brought to life, so is the other.

Go to a metaphysical store and intuitively select a crystal that you feel will enhance your dreaming. If you are unsure which one to buy, hold them separately in your hand until you find one which makes your body tingle all over. Before you go to sleep at night, place the crystal on your forehead and enter into a dreamscape from your past, a world you visited in sleep that is still in your memory.

The places we travel through in dreams, no matter how dark or scary, always carry some sort of healing force, because we created them; they are the medicine of our sleeping bodies. Venture into one of these dreamscapes and stay there as long as you want, recalling your favorite scenes as though you were watching a movie. Then, when you are ready for sleep, remove the crystal and doze off.

After a while, the crystal will start to carry the energy of your dreams. When you put it on at night, it will awaken your memory, realign the necessary circuits, so that in the morning, you will remember your dreams. Place it next to your bed in a box or on a stand. Sleep is a sacred activity. The crystal will be your reminder.

◎ Invoking Psychic Dreams

As soon as you are regularly remembering your dreams, you can begin calling forth psychic dreams. The first step in invoking a psychic dream is to think of a question you want answered, something about your future that you wish your soul to advise you on. Should I leave my job? Am I going to meet a new lover? What is my next novel going to be about? Should I have children?

Every night before you fall asleep, hold the question in your body. Feel all the different sensations the question carries. Sometimes our most urgent questions arise from hidden fears that have nothing to do with what we are asking. The desire to move to another city, for instance, might stem from a feeling of inadequacy or sadness with the life we have created. We might want the change, the excitement, the rush of a new beginning, to avoid all the pain and regret that is moving inside us.

Before you ask the question, lie with it, exploring it all the way to the roots. Do this for two or three nights, until you are absolutely certain this is the question you want to ask. Then, on the night you feel ready, envision the question rising out of your body like a sacrament to the heavens. At the same time, perform some steady slow breathing. How you enter sleep determines to a great extent how your dreams will come to you. Entering sleep like a meditation, from a still, focused body, will make your evening travels more transparent.

More than likely you will not receive an answer to the question the following morning. It will probably take a few days or a week until you get a clear and intelligible response. Nevertheless, ask the question each night like a prayer before going to sleep. This will not only help you invoke a psychic dream, but also teach you more about the questions you are asking, about what they really mean to you. Who knows, the answer might come to you before you fall asleep, as you are waiting on the edge of your pillow, a gift from the gods!

ⓦ Dream Voices

With some psychic dreams, there is no need for interpretation. You will hear a voice superimposed over the images that tells you exactly what you need to hear. Either that, or the message will be spoken through one of the characters in your dream. A gas station attendant might advise you not to take a certain trip, or a dream figure that looks like your mother will notify you about the imminent death of one of your relatives. Upon waking, you will know exactly what the dream means. The words will be ringing in your ears. There will be no mystery. The answer will be right inside you.

It is important when this happens to go into a quiet place in yourself and listen to the words several times as they move through your body. There might be some other impressions you are meant to receive—insights, pictures, memories—that will further instruct you on how to use the information.

Not all of the messages we receive in our dreams are meant for public consumption. Trust your intuition about how you should act upon what you've heard. If you witnessed in your dream that your son is going to be abandoned by his girlfriend, maybe just being more loving and close to your child is the best thing you can do. Follow your instincts. There are many ways you can use your dream insights without breathing a word.

Dreams come in stages. Often the part that arrives at night is only the first chapter. Other dimensions of the dream will meet you during the day, or later that week, as part of your private musings, while you are washing the dishes, driving your car, knitting. If you want, write the messages you receive in your journal, or on a large piece of paper. Keeping a log of your dreams will inspire your soul to stay in contact, to speak to you more frequently.

Sometimes a dream voice will tell you something that has nothing to do with the questions you asked, or even your own life. Information about your friends, your school, your town, your country will come flooding into your sleep. See if you can figure out how these insights are related to your life. Dreams are, to some degree, always personal. Listen for clues. Be creative.

◎ How to Find Psychic Messages in a Dream

Interpreting dreams, whether they are psychic or not, is always a little tricky. Dreams are not statistical. You cannot just look them up in a book and get a regimented answer. Dreams are more like art. They can be studied from numerous angles. You can probe a dream for a whole year and receive dozens of insights, messages, clues. A single dream can reveal an entire personality, a karmic struggle that will manifest itself in some form or another until the end of a person's life.

In order to derive psychic messages from a dream, you need to evaluate each image, color, sound, and fluctuation of mood and feeling. You need to go back into the dreamscape the way a detective visits a crime scene, researching exactly what happened, what each character's intentions were, when the feelings in the dream originated in your life, and how they are being played out in the present.

The psychic part of the dream is the part that guides you in a new direction, that heals you and shows you a more advanced way of living that is in harmony with your soul's path. To uncover this layer of the dream you need to focus on aspects of the dream that really touch your heart. Everything we see in our dreams has multiple layers. The surface images are like wrapped gifts; they need to be opened, studied, transformed. By sitting and contemplating any single facet of your dream—a symbol, a color, a mood—you will allow psychic insights to rise into your consciousness. There are some video adventure games that operate on this premise. Only after you touch a tree four times with your walking stick will the gnome standing behind it appear in your vision; or after you put your foot into an icy lake, a set of marble stairs will appear that lead into an underwater palace. Dreams have the same shape-shifting imagery. Anything you explore in-depth, through meditation, painting, poetry, will change as you touch it, provide you with unseen messages that guide you in your waking life.

The other night I had a dream in which I was sitting at a picnic table with a group of people. When I wasn't looking, my friend added an extra piece of meat to my plate. This made me happy. It felt wonderful that someone was so concerned for my well-being. But when I touched the meat, I discovered that it was not as well-cooked as the other pieces I had been eating. The meat was more raw and difficult to eat.

When I woke up, I had the feeling that the dream carried some important psychic message. I came to the understanding that the meat symbolized the nourishment my friend provides me with, which is not always easy to take. His love reaches all the way back to my childhood, forcing me to face parts of myself that are still broken.

All dreams have psychic attributes. You just have to look for them, letting your intuition expose the hidden layers. A good time to recall your dreams is when you are engaged in an activity in which you feel relaxed and mindful. Let your dreams have a voice in your day, and sure enough you will begin to perceive hidden psychic elements that relate to your life.

In the book *Man and His Symbols*, Carl Jung says this about dream analysis:

> ... *it is plain foolishness to believe in ready made systematic guides to dream interpretation, as if one could simply buy a reference book and look up a particular symbol. No dream*

symbol can be separated from the individual who dreams it, and there is no definite or straightforward interpretation of any dream . . .

Jung wrote this at the end of his life, after studying dreams with thousands of patients. His research had brought him full circle. Dreams were once again a personal phenomenon.

Above all, trust yourself to interpret the psychic data of a dream. Remember, in the sleeping world even the most disparate ideas can be related. A nightmare could carry in it a prediction about your grandmother's health. Be open to the zany and the profound, the yin and yang, the light and dark in every dreamscape you journey through.

Dreams are as stimulating to interpret as Shakespeare's plays. You can work on them alone or with friends. They are rich in metaphor and universal meaning. When you bring them into your daily life, they will feed you, help you join the right and left sides of your brain, and expand your vision.

◎ Photographic Psychic Dreams

There are some psychic dreams in which you see something happen with unusual clarity, and then a week, a month, or a year later, the event happens in real life. In these dreams, we move into the position of the witness. We are not really part of the dream. We are a bystander, observing something pass before us with the lucidity of everyday life.

When you wake up from one of these dreams, there will be a knowing in your body that transcends interpretation. You will feel as though you had a vision rather than a dream. Often, though, we forget these dreams, and then experience them later as *déjà vus*. We walk into a store and see an old friend, and our body registers the feeling that we have already experienced this moment.

A psychic dream can forecast the most mundane event—taking a trip to a shoe store in your yellow sweatsuit—or the most intense happening, such as the death of a loved one or a fatal accident. You may feel an eerie chill upon waking. Sometimes these dreams will even throw you out of sleep, causing you to rise in your bed in the middle of the night sweating and breathing heavily.

Most of us are not used to being in such close contact with our soul. We might observe a character in a movie who has this ability, or read about it in books, but when it happens to us, we are emotionally terrified. My advice for these moments is to rejoice. Even if you feel jolted, disoriented, alarmed, thank the gods they have given you such a broad vision of your life. As Rilke said, "We have no reason to mistrust our world. Has it terrors, they are our terrors. Has it abysses, they belong to us." All the things that frighten us are part of our being. Feeling scared of a psychic dream is like a bird being scared of his wings. We are deep, vast creatures. When you are blessed with a night vision, accept it. With time, you will learn to handle it better, to use this connection as a means of guidance for yourself and those around you.

Again, trust yourself with whether or not you should share what you have witnessed in your dream. We are never obligated to be a messiah. If there is a way you can save someone from a deadly accident or illness, by all means speak out, but otherwise, if you see pain or heartbreak in someone's future, the best thing you can do may simply be to pray for him. Go into a silent space in yourself and send him light. Often this will touch a person's life more deeply than words. Listen to the empath, and she will guide you to a wise choice.

Photographic psychic dreams often come to us when we are at a crossroads, when our soul is shedding its skin and preparing for a new life. The dreams will flash through our sleep like quick documentaries, more vivid in color and sound than our regular dreams. Such a dream can be precipitated by asking a question before you fall asleep, or it may come unannounced, like a stone hurled at your window. When you invite them into your life consciously, they will arrive with more grace. You are prepared. Your body is ready.

Judith Orloff writes extensively about psychic dreams in her book *Second Sight*. She says that the more healed you are inside, the more issues you have resolved from your childhood, the clearer your channel will be to receive psychic dreams. If your dreams are not coming to you in this manner, don't worry about it. Just keep exploring the dreams that are in your life right now, delving into them for psychic information. When the time is right, your consciousness will shift to accommodate more direct transmissions. There is no rush. When you are ready, your dreaming abilities will grow.

My spiritual counselor told me something in one of our sessions that really affected me. She said that only a few of us wish to know things straight up. The majority of people prefer to be ignorant, to not see, to live in a fog. It is easier that way. When the messages you receive are crystal clear, you have no choice but to face your fears, to follow your real life. Psychic dreams will move you into this position. When an important decision arises, you will know exactly what to do. The labyrinth will be filled with light.

The author Carlos Castaneda said there are two types of people, dreamers and stalkers. Stalkers have dreams that are usually quite abstract, dreams that need to be probed for meaning. Stalkers' insights usually come more during the day, when they are out in the world pursuing their goals. Dreamers are the opposite. Guidance comes to them most clearly at night. Their dreams are lucid and precise.

My sister is a dreamer. Since she was a young girl, she has been able to be conscious in her sleep, to steer herself through her dreams like a mermaid through the water. For me, dreaming has always been more like a ride at the fair. I just strap myself into bed and hang on for the ride. I am a stalker. Slowly I am learning the arts of her world, and she of mine.

Stop for a second and think about yourself. Into which category do you fit more accurately? Are you a dreamer or a stalker? Give yourself a few moments to meditate on your dreaming life. Write down in your notebook some of your most memorable dreams, and describe what they gave you, what they taught you about your soul's path.

Is there a dream you had in childhood that foreshadowed your life's purpose? A future mate? Buy yourself a dream journal and promise yourself to document all your nightly travels. Be consistent. Just writing your dreams will open your psychic life.

There are some people who believe we have multiple roles, that we might be a carpenter during the day, but while we are sleeping, our soul is employed somewhere else. One of my sister's teachers says that at night she helps people die and be reborn into other dimensions. This, too, can be part of our dreaming. Ask your soul where you go during sleep. Write down what you hear. Who are you at night? Who are you when you dream?

Psychic Relationships

It is all an open secret.
—RAMANA MAHARASHI

 In our society, the one place it is socially acceptable to be a psychic empath is in a relationship. Once we have known someone for many years, slept together, shared food, gone to movies, cried, laughed, there is an intimacy that develops in which we can share ourselves without words, without cumbersome explanations. Whether we are in the same room or in different countries, our channels are open to each other; we are wired, fused, entwined. A psychic relationship can happen with anyone—your friend, your lover, your sister, your mother. The only prerequisite is that your souls touch, that the invisible part of your beings receive each other with love and understanding.

Since I have been doing readings professionally, I have come upon hundreds of people who are able to connect with each other in this manner. As I am performing a reading, I will see my clients sending each other signals back and forth like spiritual masters. They won't even be aware they are doing it. It is instinctual, swift, unconscious.

If my reading is accurate, they might ask me when it's finished, "God, how do you do that? How can you know so much about my life?" Meanwhile, they were projecting and receiving information with the same clarity and precision I was. When I tell them this, they usually laugh and shrug off what I said as flattery. For many, the word "psychic" is so big, so titanic, they can't accept it. They don't realize it is a normal state of being, that as a parent, a lover, and a friend, we use this part of ourselves all the time.

When we are psychic with a person we love, we think it is ordinary. When we are psychic with a stranger, we think it is magic. Really, it's the same thing. We've just been conditioned to believe that the intuition we share with the people close to us is a different phenomenon, a less powerful one. It isn't. At a certain level, all human beings have a thread between them, a line from soul to soul. When you feel safe with someone, relaxed and affectionate, you are more inclined to touch this thread. But it is always there. Between you and the cashier at the grocery store, you and your neighbor, you and a stranger on the bus. The Internet is simply an externalization of the intuitive network that already connects the whole world, body to body. E-mail has been happening for millions of years.

Of all the people I have sat with, the psychic relationship I remember most vividly existed between two Asian women in their early twenties. While I was reading the cards, these two women were having a complete psychic conversation, words and thoughts moving between them in thin beams of light. When I told them what I saw, they giggled. They were surprised I had noticed what was going on. Their communication was so subtle that no one had noticed it before. I had uncovered their secret.

Of course, in my work, I have also witnessed relationships in which there is absolutely zero psychic communication. I see this with a lot of married couples. They have stopped talking. There is a dead zone between them. Out of some fear, or some hidden trauma, they have become strangers to each other, remote and unfeeling. In my readings, I usually receive the message that they should meditate together, do things that reawaken their empathic bond and bring them into a parallel world.

A lot of men I give readings to have also fallen into this trap. They have become logic addicts, locked in a prison of rational thoughts. Some women enter this state as well, but usually they don't allow themselves to get as isolated as men do. Women know in their bodies that closeness is important, that secret feelings must be transmitted in order for love to grow.

When we block ourselves from being in psychic contact with the ones we love, life inevitably becomes very lonely. It is not just spiritually rewarding but also necessary to our survival to be soulfully connected with other human beings. Privacy is important, but so is deep communion. It feeds us; it gives us the stamina we need to endure our solitude.

Later in the chapter I will show you a ritual you can do to invoke more psychic relationships in your life, and deepen the ones you already have. If you can, think of a psychic relationship not as something far out and wizardly, but simply as another stage of love, a level of intimacy where the unspoken, the unsaid, the mysterious, can travel from your body to another body without any mental interference.

There are modes of communication aside from speaking in which the light we carry can move between us and assuage our loneliness. To all who are reading this right now, I send you a greeting from this place. Here there are no walls, no dividers, no distance. Here we are all one. Here there is just love.

◉ The Psychic Heart

When we fall in love, either romantically or as friends, we take some of the other's cells into our body. Every time we talk on the phone, eat lunch, drive together in the car, there is an energetic exchange in which he or she becomes part of our consciousness. Deepak Chopra observes that just through our breath alone we have inherited two million atoms of the Buddha and Christ. When you love someone, this process happens tenfold. That is why couples who have been together for a long time start to look like each other. Their cells begin to replicate in similar patterns. They empathically take on each other's physical and psychological characteristics.

A meditation teacher once said that when we are interacting with someone on an intimate level, the part of us that stays the same, the core of our identity, is actually smaller than the part of us that changes. This is even more true if we are involved sexually. When we make love, our bodies explode into each other, becoming a cloud of shared electrons. That is why it is not healthy to be promiscuous. On a psychic level, it is disorienting to share one's body with too many people.

In order to develop psychic relationships, you need to become more conscious of how the people you love live inside your body, how their thoughts and feelings move through your being. There is a specific emotional landscape inside us that represents our connection with another person. The more we love someone, the more this area expands. Whenever we are together or have this individual in our thoughts, our awareness shifts to the part of our psyche that we have both created. We change. As the Buddhists say, when you are with your wife, it is not you and your wife, it is you/wife. Don't mistake this for codependence. What I am speaking of is harmony, the invisible law that draws two instruments into a single field of music. In love, this synthesis happens all the time.

There is a map inside our body of all the relationships we have ever had, a tangible inner geography of all our intimate bonds. Exploring these regions we can encounter the presence of everyone we have ever loved, and if we want, unite with them, and feel their presence. Whether they are with us in the same room or traveling in a different world doesn't matter. Just by entering into ourselves we can interact with all those who have touched our soul.

Some of the meeting points inside us produce painful feelings, and others send us into bliss, depending on the state of the relationship. How a person feels in our body informs us of whether or not the bond needs healing, how the relationship is affecting our emotional and spiritual development. Even after someone passes away, he is still inside us. Whatever parts of him we need to confront or be in communion with, we can just reach into our cells and experience. There is no distance. The karma we have with those close to us is right inside our bodies. All we have to do is turn inward and face the music.

The old expression "Absence makes the heart grow fonder" is also based on this principle of inner union. When lovers are apart from each other, their souls become acquainted on a deeper, intuitive level, making the love they feel for each other more intense. Rumi says, "Lovers don't finally meet somewhere, they're in each other all along." Every psychic relationship we have has been circulating through our bodies for eons. That is why when we meet the person in the flesh, we feel that we have known him or her before. We have. They were already inside us.

Knowing this truth, a lot of profound intimacy and healing can take place simply by focusing on the presence of another person as he or she exists in our physical being. It's like having a psychic

E-mail address for each person you care for. When you want to work on the relationship, forgive her for something, feel close, send her a message, you can move into the place in your body in which you are connected, and give or receive whatever is needed. Then, when you see the person next, you are able to interact from a deeper source. The love is stronger. You are able to say things that before were too difficult to express.

The best time to explore this realm is before sleep. There is an openness in our bodies in the late evening that enables us to slide more easily into union with those we love. That is why most romance happens at night. The boundaries are thinner, the veil less concrete.

Here is the ritual I use in my life. Try it. It will serve you well.

As you are lying in bed preparing for sleep, bring into your mind the image of a person you are wanting to be close to. Visualize some moment you were together where things were really good, no distractions, total harmony. Place your hands on your chest. Stay there for a few moments and cherish the details, the sensations, the feelings.

See if you can determine in your body where you and the person meet. Is it a head relationship? Do you meet in the heart, the stomach, the third eye? Some of the relationships we have are well balanced. They consume all of us, activating our whole bodies. Others are more limited, staying focused on a particular activity or state of being.

Knowing where in the body you and another person interact gives you the choice either to accept the relationship as it is or push it into a new realm. Sometimes it is good to mix things up, to take a philosopher friend to a football game or a business partner to a yoga class. Often we don't know the full spectrum of a relationship until we move it into unexplored terrain.

Stay focused on the part of your body where you and the person meet until you can feel their presence humming inside you. When you get stuck, keep going back to memories of when you and the person were together. Visualize what he looks like when he talks, how he laughs and smiles, the light in his eyes when he is happy. Feel his mannerisms float through your being, igniting feelings in you as though he were with you in the room.

When you are ready, transmit to him whatever it is you wish

him to receive—something you have been wanting to tell him, a ray of love, laughter, or forgiveness. Use this moment to say everything you want to say. Converse with him as if he were sitting across from you in a chair listening attentively. You might be surprised with what comes out of you, what sentences are waiting in your heart.

Also, if there is something you want in return—a spark, a tickle, a warm gesture—feel yourself taking it in. I do this when I miss my father. I feel his hand on my shoulder, smell his Old Spice cologne drifting through the air. This activates the cellular memory in me in which he is still alive, still on the planet giving me his attention and care. A lot of us have an easy time giving love, but a hard time receiving it. Determine which is more difficult for you, and work to heal the imbalance.

If you are single and waiting for a mate, you can use this ritual to make contact with the lover that lives inside you that you have yet to meet in the flesh. Follow the exact same steps. Since you probably won't have any real memories to focus on, make them up. Use fantasy to awaken the connection that is already alive in your being. Doing this will help summon the person into your life, open the necessary channels so that he or she may respond to the call.

The more you do this exercise, the more you will realize how time and space are nothing more than concepts. You will start to feel close to your loved ones no matter where they are. They will be with you all the time, as near to you as your own skin.

This ritual is especially helpful during times in a relationship when conversation isn't working. Taking some time each night to focus on the person you love will help you carve a pathway of intuitive feeling, so that when you are together, you will be able to interact with less difficulty.

If for some reason you are spending large amounts of time away from someone you love, you could arrange to do this exercise at the same time every day, creating an empathic bridge to sweeten your separation. My wife and I did this when she was in France for two months doing a play. We had long-distance meetings from body to body. It was not as good as the real thing, but it made the distance more bearable.

Once you get familiar with this ritual, it will start to happen on its own. Whoever you are meant to be in contact with that day will appear inside you. Ask yourself, why am I feeling this or that person today? Do they need me? Do I need them? Are they all right?

Parents experience this all the time. A father could be sitting on the beach in Tahiti and feel his son's heartbreak all the way up in New York City. A mother may feel a pain in her arm when her child falls from a horse. The more we love someone, the more psychic energy passes between us. It is the way of nature. The more you allow it, the clearer the connection becomes.

Final note. If you want, you can use this ritual to communicate with parts of yourself from the past: the curious toddler, the lonely adolescent, the confused twenty-year-old. With the way our culture has shifted in the last hundred years, many people have had difficult beginnings, gotten lost on their path to adulthood and never uncovered their particular gift. Using your empathic ability, you can go back in time and heal yourself, be your own savior, your own guide.

Take some time to remember when it was you really needed a friend, a teacher, or a parent and didn't have one. Go there and talk with yourself. Travel through time. Give your light to the one who needs it the most. You.

SEVEN MORE WAYS TO AWAKEN THE EMPATH

1. The empath sees people as stories, a river of events with no fixed points, all overlapping and mixing together. When you meet people, allow yourself to perceive all of them, from the child all the way to the elder. At each moment, we act from a different age, a different space in our being. Be watchful. Forget time. See all of someone's life in a single frame.

2. When you feel comfortable, share with people what you feel they were like as children, what their gifts were, whether they were shy, boisterous, clumsy, spoiled. Trust your feelings. It is natural for us to sense the child in each other. When we do, another world opens, one in which we feel more sensitive, more in tune with how to give love to those around us.

3. Be constantly listening to your moment-to-moment needs, when you need to drink a glass of water, go for a walk, stop talking,

see a movie, relax in nature. The main purpose of our intuition is to take care of ourselves, to nurture our body and be attentive to what our soul is craving. When you get confused, ask your inner voice. The empath guides us in simple ways, one step at a time, leading us to greater mental, physical, and spiritual health.

4. As much as you can, avail yourself of various methods of healing: massage, therapy, acupressure, t'ai chi, hot baths. The more you listen, the more your body will lead the way, showing you exactly what suits your temperament. You will wake up in the morning, and your back will cry out for oil and Swedish hands, or your heart will say, "God, I need to talk to someone." Always say yes. In the modern world, we need healing all the time. Try everything once. The empath knows exactly when to make the call.

5. Open yourself to the intelligence of plants and animals. Spend time meditating under a tree or by the river. Pretend you are a tribal guide, and take a hike strictly by following your intuition, the sounds of birds, insects, the wind. Get to know nature as an extension of your body, from the clouds in the sky to the crabs on the beach. It is easier to read people and your environment when you feel things as part of your being. Nature will teach you this, how to dissolve boundaries and merge with everything.

6. Reach out to people with love in the moment you feel they need it, with a phone call, a letter, a touch on the shoulder. Let the empath guide you, telling you when to slip your light into another person's world. Make the point of being with children as much as you can. Children are wildly psychic. They will teach you a lot about feelings, intuition, the grace of living with an open heart.

7. Sit with a close friend or lover and stare into his eyes for two minutes, sending him as much love as you can with your whole body. During these two minutes, he should think of nothing but receiving, of being healed by the light of your gaze. Then switch.

When you are done, tell each other what perceptions appeared through this channel of grace.

PART IV

Summoning the Warrior

Moment by Moment

There is always another time, another second, another hour
to do it right.

The reason a lot of us make poor life decisions is that we
are not practiced at making good moment-to-moment
decisions. We run our lives on cruise control, like a
toy train whizzing around a circular track. When we
get to a crossroads, and have to make a choice between path a, b,
or c, we feel crushed. We don't trust ourselves to make the right
decision. We panic, call our friends, our therapist, our psychic. We
need outside advice, another person to make the move for us.

To overcome this problem, we need to bring the warrior into
our daily lives, moment by moment, until we become comfortable
having the reins in our own hands. You can develop your instincts
every second of the day—while scanning the grocery aisle for dinner, socializing at a party, or browsing at a bookstore. When you
use your intuition to make simple choices—what movie to see,
what person to talk to at a party—your soul will start to work
through you to manifest your dreams. It's like buying houses in a
Monopoly game. After three or four instinctual moves, you have
a hotel on Boardwalk, a synchronistic event that will expand your
life and help you move to the next level.

From selecting the right book, you might attend the right

seminar, meet the right business partner, start the right company, and presto, your life has advanced. What holds most of us back from surrendering to this natural rhythm is fear of the unknown. We want to know why we are doing something and what it will get us, rather than just trusting our instincts and waiting to see what happens.

The day you enter a bookstore and find yourself drawn to a volume about Zen, you question it. Yesterday you didn't have an interest in Japanese philosophy. Why are you interested today? You are American, not Japanese. Are you ill? Is there something wrong with you? You turn around and head to the mystery section and buy your fifteenth technothriller. It feels comfortable in your hands. Little do you know that it will set into motion the same pattern of thoughts you had yesterday, the ones that made you stay home and feel helpless waiting for your true love to come. As you get in your car, you have already forgotten the fresh impulse that passed through you only minutes ago. The Zen book is still on the shelf. You drive away.

We have all been this person at some time or another—a slave to advertising, old habits, unresolved fears. In moderation, this style of living is okay. It is restful and keeps us feeling relaxed and safe. But when our need for security becomes overdeveloped and we stop breaking into new worlds, our antennae start to go dead. After a while, our intuition disappears.

To keep our psychic juices flowing, we need to respond to new signals, to open new doors. Even a small detour can have an impact on our life. Each day we are given opportunities to expand our instinctual nature, to reach beyond our limitations and enhance our ourselves and the planet. Living this way requires moment-by-moment navigation, daring and playful leaps outside of our comfort zones.

As an Aries, I can be quite stubborn when I want to be. On the Fourth of July last year my wife had the feeling that we should go to a friend's party in Malibu. I wanted to see a movie instead. The idea of following her intuition made me crazy. I became a pouting child. As we drove up the coastal highway, I did nothing but complain. Finally she gave in to my will. Another Aries trait: When we want something, we don't stop.

Outside the theater, I felt a heaviness in my body, a feeling that something was off. I looked over at her. "You're right," I said. "We are meant to go to the party. This isn't it."

It turned out to be a tremendous evening. We arrived in Malibu just in time to see the fireworks displays of Barbra Streisand and Danny DeVito competing for our attention. Later, at the party, we met a couple who had been together for twenty-two years. The four of us had an instant rapport. They were the ultimate model of how two people can live together, pursue their art, have children, and still remain independent, wild human beings. I thoroughly enjoyed their presence. I knew they had been placed in my life for a reason. They were a reflection of my future, of the life I was here to live. What a wonderful thing that I actually yielded to my and my wife's intuition. If I hadn't, the meeting would have never occurred.

The reason growth is so painful for many of us is because we put off change for years and years until sometimes it is too late. We miss thousands of opportunities to grow because we are afraid to trust our instincts and step outside of our comfort zones. Only after we get cancer or lose our spouse do we turn inward and start following the voices that have been calling to us all along. If we listen to the psychic in each moment, in ourselves and others, we can avoid a lot of grief, by doing things in the second they need to be done and moving on.

Each day is like a painting. When we get out of bed in the morning, we are faced with a blank canvas. We can make anything we want, a Rembrandt, a Picasso, a cartoon. Many of us aren't aware of this. We reach for the same brush, dip it in the same color, and add another layer to the picture we have been painting for the last ten years.

A psychic wakes up differently. She knows that today she is a different person, that she has grown during sleep, that her cells carry new information. Instead of dipping into the green she used yesterday, she plunges her brush into the pastel blue or the cherry red. She lets her instincts guide her rather than old fears. She might end up at the same office, sitting at the same desk, but she walks in fresh, knowing that within the parameters of her responsibilities, she can be whatever she wants.

Tuning in to your instincts will help you reach wholeness. If you are one of those people who spends too much time reading spiritual books, and your head is filled with dogma, one day you might feel drawn to spy novels, to a new interest that will balance your character and ground you. To live instinctually, we need to be open to new pathways of learning, and trust that what our heart is drawn to will assist us on our soul's path.

◎ Exercise

When you wake up tomorrow morning, take a minute before each activity to tune in to yourself and determine what your instincts are telling you. When you look in your closet for clothes to wear, see if you can feel what color represents your mood, what skirt or jacket matches the energy that is swimming through your body. Don't let yourself off the hook easily. If you can't figure out what impulses are coming to you, just stand there until you get a picture in your mind. Be patient. For many of us, this type of listening needs to be developed.

Do the same with your breakfast. Take a second to ask your body what it wants to eat, and in what order. If you feel that your body wants a banana and a glass of water, then give it that. Take your time. Perform your morning rituals strictly by instinct.

What if you receive the message to call in sick for work, eat a bag of doughnuts, burn all your ties, and move to Bermuda . . . what do you do then? You might be one of those people who is living so far from your authentic self that when you turn inward for guidance, you get the feeling that your life isn't yours . . .

If this happens, write down in your journal the exact ideas and impulses that came to you and determine how realistic it is that you integrate them into your life. Remember, this exercise is not about fantasy escapes. It concerns fine-tuning, how to listen moment by moment to our own basic awareness of what we need to do to stay in harmony with our soul. Most of us have grown up with poor self-esteem. We don't treat ourselves well. We don't honor our own intuition. We eat when we're not hungry. We don't get enough sleep. We wear clothes that don't suit us. Being conscious and alert with your morning rituals is a way of listening to your own inner yearning. When we do this, we feel more alive and life takes on a new and exciting perspective.

What we are doing is caretaking the four primary levels of being: mind, body, emotion, and soul. Take the time each day to find out how you can stimulate these different parts of yourself so that you develop and awaken your entire psyche for the challenges of the day.

If you are one of those people who has a family, or works nonstop in several jobs, it is even more necessary that you make time for reflection at the beginning of each day to help you stay centered. You might feel the impulse to meditate for a few seconds or take a quick walk after sending the kids to school. Even one small moment of stopping, quieting the mind, and listening to yourself can ripple out and enhance the entire day.

Later that night, when you are lying in bed, write down some notes as to how your day was affected by the choices you made in the morning. Did you get a date because of the outfit you wore? Were you more alert and less hungry because of the breakfast you ate? Were you happier without reading the paper? Was poetry a better substitute?

The effects of your morning rituals might be loud or subtle. Try doing the exercise again next week. Each time you discover something that makes you feel better, healthier, more at peace, integrate it into your life. Nobody can tell you what you need. We can only discover what is right for us through our intuition. Doing this exercise will help you get in the habit of turning inside for guidance. When we learn this skill, anything is possible.

Movement

When the right thing happens, the whole body knows.
—ROBERT BLY

 As humans, we spend a lot of our time in movement, walking, driving, running. In these moments it is just as important to be in tune with your instincts as it is while you are stationary, sitting with your friend eating lunch or painting in your studio. As you are moving, there are opportunities for intuitive navigation that can add to your day the synchronicities you need to stay in tune with your soul's path. Sometimes walking into the shop that you would never enter, or taking a different route home in your car, can mean the difference between an ordinary day and one you will never forget.

Since we have left the country for the suburbs and the city, a lot of us have lost touch with how to move in our bodies in a way that is alert and sensitive. I believe this is the reason there are so many automobile accidents every year. People have simply forgotten how to operate their bodies efficiently, with the animal awareness that was common to us when we lived closer to the earth. A lot of us move with the same awkwardness as our machines. We have lost the flow, the rhythm of the wilderness that can guide us through life.

My brother George told me that when he was visiting Jamaica he met people who could run through a pitch black jungle at midnight and barely make a sound. They could do it with their eyes closed, jumping over logs and streams, dodging trees. This is how amazing our bodies are. When we give them the attention and care they need, they can help steer us through the world with the least possible effort. Our bodies are vastly intelligent. They have radars and guidance systems beyond our wildest imagination, for they are part of nature, and nature is always in motion.

For instance, Canadian geese have a navigational ability that leads them each year on a migratory path from the northern states to Central America with the precision of a modern aircraft. The Aborigines of Australia (who are sometimes referred to as the real people) can track freshwater springs that are seven or eight feet underground through the soles of their feet. In a barren desert, these people know exactly which way to travel, where to dig in the sand to find dinner by pure instinct alone.

These modes of awareness are available to all of us. One way to activate them is to learn movement all over again, to experience yourself in motion with the same curiosity and wonder as when you were two years old. When you do this, you become in sync with the same forces that guide an eagle to perch on a certain cliff, or an acorn to land on a particular spot of ground. Evolutionary tracts open up. Senses are awakened that have been sleeping for a thousand years.

In the next part of this chapter, I will show you various ways to make your movement more psychic, from walking, to driving, to dancing. When we stop taking these states of being for granted, and learn to be more mindful in the simplest moments, then our travels on the planet can be intuitive every step of the way. This chapter is about moving back in time, not forward. This is where the answers are, in the great silences before civilization occurred, the old roads, the old footsteps. This is where we all need to go.

⊚ Moving in the Mind

Fantasizing in your mind how you would like to move in your body enhances your instincts. I had a therapist named Kay Links who gave me sessions from her wheelchair. When she was a girl, Kay had wanted to be a ballerina. She joked sometimes that, after her death, I should keep my eyes open for beautiful young dancers. In the next round, this is what she was going to be. Kay passed away two years ago. Since then, my eyes are always on the lookout for young Margot Fonteyns.

Even though I never saw Kay do a pirouette or a leap, she had a grace in her that was phenomenal. The way she opened a soda, rubbed her hands together, caressed her arm, was fluid and effortless. Kay was one of those rare people who could speak and move with the timing of her soul. She was psychic in her every action. Her words, like a blaze of fire, exposed you to the core at exactly the right moment, so that you could see your problem in full view and change it.

A lot of her precision and timing, I believe, came from spending hours and hours dreaming of herself on the stage under the lights, spiraling and flowing with the music. Even though she was dead from the waist down, she had brought the dancer into her body, inspired in herself a rich intuition from her fantasies alone.

When you are feeling stiff and out of tune with your instincts, lie down somewhere and visualize effortless movement. Maybe you are an animal: a cat, a raven, or an elk. Perhaps your movement has the crescendo of a crashing wave or the wildness of leaping flames. See what style of movement comes to you, what physical language expresses your soul.

Try to remember all of the bodies you have wanted to have since you were a child, from Baryshnikov to Plastic Man. Create from these bodies one that it is uniquely your own. Imagine this body moving in your mind, climbing stairs, dancing, making love, gliding into all the spheres of life you are afraid you will never enter, the executive office, the hockey rink, the opera house.

Give the body a color and let it rush through your being. Maybe you just need this body for the day, for a tennis match with your friend, or maybe this is the body you want for your life, the one strong and reliable enough to carry out your soul's path.

See this body moving through time, at different ages, strong, healthy, loving. If you want, draw a picture of this body and put it on your wall, or write a poem about it, describing it from the inside out.

Visualize the body in your mind during any awkward or clumsy moment when you need grace, instinct, timing. Use the body as a reference point, a symbol of what it is like when your soul and flesh are one.

The body I see in myself is firm and grounded, and at the same time, weightless and full of light. It has the quickness of a jaguar and the fluidity of water. It doesn't ask permission to move. It doesn't freeze up at crucial moments. It is always free.

What is your body like? Are you bold enough to use it, to be that beautiful? In what way will it serve you better than the body you are using now? What do you need to do to make this body real?

Follow your heart. This is not a *Cosmo* quiz. Go beyond appearance. See the body as a manifestation of how you move on the inside, the way in which your spirit takes form when it enters your skin. You might not be as docile as you think. Your real body might caress like the wind, or shine with a child's enthusiasm.

In his book *Quantum Healing,* Deepak Chopra says that in a year we replace ninety-eight percent of the cells in our body. Visualization is one of the ways in which this process occurs. Dream your real body. Carry the image of effortless movement everywhere you go, and without a doubt, you will always flow into the right place at the right time.

◉ Walking

Humans have been walking for thousands of years. It's our natural milieu. Before we had cars and airplanes, walking was how we investigated the world, hunted, shopped, traveled. Philosophers such as Emerson and Rousseau used walking as a counterbalance to their writing, to probe deeply into ideas and enlighten their work. When you bring more awareness into your walking, it excites the instinctual channels in your body, making you alert to events before they happen: accidents, crimes, chance meetings.

Each time we walk, it's a brand new experience. A trip to the corner store can be as interesting as passing through a market in Egypt. On a bright Sunday morning you could meet an old friend or your soul mate. When you go out walking, you face life head on. Their is no shield around you. You are moving through the wilderness.

I have always been a walker. When given the choice, I always travel on foot. When I am walking, I am not alone. There are other walkers with me—Buddha, Gandhi, the African tribeswoman with the wooden jug on her head. Walking is a vast continuum. If you are open, you can feel the presence of a lot of other travelers. This is why I like to walk. It brings me out of time and connects me with other great beings.

One thing my father taught me was to be aware of my posture as I walked. When you walk with a straight spine, from the top of your head to your lower back, your magnetic field expands. Being hunched over blocks the sensors in your body. You become disconnected from your surroundings. Walking with a straight posture and a relaxed open chest widens your perceptions, allowing you to pick up subtle psychic messages as they flow into your awareness.

Breath is also important. When you are breathing well, you become more in tune with what is around you. Look at a deer. It is partly because of their sensitive breathing that they can sense your hiking boots scuff gravel a mile down the path. When you are walking, keep your breath deep and steady. It will refine your instincts.

Speed is another thing to consider. I learned this right away in New York. There are some streets in the Big Apple that are not meant for strolling. Paris, on the other hand, encourages you to slow down, loosen the hips, carry a parasol and a journal. Each landscape has its own music. When you are walking, see if you can sense in your body what pace is calling you, what rhythm and mood.

When a Masai warrior crosses the desert, he lopes like a timber wolf. In the bush, he moves with the slowness of a praying mantis. Be like the Masai. Merge with your environment. It will open you up to the signals you are meant to hear, and make your walking more profound.

Look at the horizon when you walk, rather than at the ground in front of you. It gives you a broader vision of life. Keep your eyes on the treetops and buildings rather than the cracks in the sidewalk. See what it does to your state of mind.

Some of my best psychic insights have come to me while walking. If you want, bring a Dictaphone with you when you walk. Talk to yourself at certain points on the voyage, while you are standing under a tree, waiting for the bus, or crossing a bridge. Often we are more receptive to intuitive ideas when we are outside the house, away from the television and the air conditioner. Let your soul speak to you. See what it has to say.

In the movie *Dead Poets Society,* there is a scene in which a teacher takes his students outside and invites them all to find their own walk. When your soul and body are one, how do you move? There is only one John Wayne. What is your stride?

◎ Driving

Let's face it, we live in a modern age. We have to drive. In a few centuries, we may have our time machines and strap-on helicopters, but for now, it's the automobile. For most of us, driving is a way of life.

What a better time to practice being psychic than behind the wheel. If there is ever a need for a Nostradamus insight, it is when you are cruising along at sixty miles an hour in a flow of pushy traffic. This is where being clairvoyant really counts. It could save your life.

I owe this section to my friend Lorin Roche. Lorin is a meditation teacher. It is part of his genius to find ways to be alert and conscious while in the throes of modern living. If it weren't for him, I'd still be driving with my third eye closed. What he taught me has seriously changed my driving habits, and made me as competent with a stick shift as I am with Tarot cards. Here is his advice:

1. Before you get in the car, check your emotional state. Don't take your frustration or your anger with you. Be conscious of where you are going and why you are going there. If your destination can be reached by a means other than driving, consider an alternate mode of transportation. On the one day that I decided to walk ten blocks to the post office rather than drive, I met an old friend I had not seen for a long time, who taught me some much-needed guitar chords which enhanced my song writing. It was well worth the twenty extra minutes of travel time. When you move at a primitive speed, you experience more of life. Think before you drive. Consider your alternatives.

2. Before you start your car, visualize your destination. See yourself already there, happy, refreshed, all of your passengers in one piece. Then imagine around your body a field of protective energy, an orb of light shielding you from dangerous events. When you are ready, pull out of your space slowly and mindfully. Most accidents happen a mile from home. Be awake the whole time.

3. Once you are on the street, feel a chord of magnetism reaching from the base of your spine into the concrete. Feel yourself centered on this chord. Feel it straightening your posture and making your whole body brim with alertness.

As you are driving, keep this connection with the ground. Don't focus all of your attention here, just enough so that you feel the presence of the road beneath you, like a streetcar wire to which you are electrically fused. Doing this will align your chakras and give you a 360-degree awareness of the road. Your body will see things before your eyes do. You'll be fully aware behind the wheel.

4. Travel at a speed that doesn't interfere with your intuition, a speed at which you can monitor everything around you, and at the same time, stay focused on the road. See if you can feel instinctually when you have reached this speed without looking at your speedometer. When we listen closely, the body gives us psychic cues. Take this as an opportunity to get in touch with your instincts, to learn what it is like to experience movement through your feeling nature.

5. Allow a comfortable space between yourself and other cars. As my friend Lorin puts it, "Own a piece of the street." Be a territorial driver. Not in a dangerous way, but as a mode of safety, like tending your own section of the garden. This will activate all the sensors in your body and make the field of space surrounding your car charged with psychic energy. When anything hazardous is about to enter this area, your body will notify you immediately. It will be like a weed trying to overtake your roses. The soil will tremble. You'll be able to slow down, switch lanes, change streets, just in time to prevent an accident.

6. Trust your instincts moment by moment. If you get the feeling that you need to stop for a second, change your route, accelerate, or slow down, do so immediately. Be conscious every second of how your automobile wants to be driven. Let your psychic mind direct you the whole time.

The warrior maintains order, balance, and serenity in the most chaotic of situations. When we are driving, we are at our most lethal. More than ever do we need to be conscious of exactly what we are doing. Applying these six steps will make your driving more intuitive and aware. When you get on the road, you'll be prepared for whatever comes your way.

One final suggestion: Go for a psychic drive once a month. Just get in your car and drive, using your intuition as your guide. Visit places you wouldn't normally visit: shops, parks, cafés. Get used to what it feels like to move by instinct alone, and see where you end up.

⊚ Dancing

A big part of being psychic is having an open body, a clear channel through which your soul may express itself. Dance helps us cultivate this openness. It frees up our inhibitions, and gives us the suppleness and flexibility we need to stay in tune with our soul's path.

In some old societies, they wouldn't give a warrior a sword until he could dance. When we free the dancer in us, our movement comes more from the heart. We have less resistance to love; there is more joy and enthusiasm in our bodies.

There is no way I could possibly teach you in this book how to dance. That would be ridiculous. I am simply suggesting this: Give yourself a few moments each day to move to music, to lose yourself in a rhythm, a melody, or primordial sounds. Allow your body to express the intuitive feelings that move through your cells. Sometimes I dance a color. I dance red, green, or yellow. Other times I dance a character, a werewolf, a tree, a clown. I use dance to invoke my soul, to incorporate new frequencies into my body.

If I have danced sometime in the day, allowed my body to melt into music, then my psychic readings are always better. It's like getting a massage before making love. When you dance, you bridge the gap between body and soul. Whatever psychic ideas want to come through you rise to the surface. You are more open, more receptive to divine inspiration.

Don't follow any rules when you dance. Surrender to the uniqueness of your own being. In tribal cultures, dancing is a way of letting the gods into your body. Think of all the wars that could have been avoided if people had danced more, or if someone had played some ABBA on the battlefield before the swords were drawn.

Dance opens the eyes on our skin. When we don't dance, part of us dies. We lose our instincts, our physical magic. Dance keeps us open to the hidden instruments, the subtle sounds that seek our expression from the other side.

If you need some inspiration, watch some videos of Fred Astaire and Ginger Rogers, or attend a Native American rain dance. Or begin dancing in your mind. See yourself twisting through space and then pull the movements into your limbs. Some of the best dancing comes out of total stillness. On the outside you may hardly be moving, but on the inside you are wild and free.

Being intuitive means being open to the Great Dance, to the part of life that transcends logic. A dancer and a psychic are one and the same. They both give expression to the invisible, taking what is not seen and drawing it into the world. When your visionary ability feels hampered, dance yourself back into life. Let the movement of your body liberate your instinctual nature. Put on a good song and let it all happen.

We each have a style of movement in which we are most psychic. A client of mine named Sydney says that on the ground his intuition is so-so, but when he is flying his plane, he becomes completely clairvoyant, able to predict weather patterns with the sensitivity of a bird. For my friend Lorin, it is the motion of swimming that opens his deepest awareness. When he is in the ocean, his senses become totally refined. He can communicate with other beings— seals, dolphins, underwater plants. For me it has always been skiing. Since I was young, whenever I am on the slopes, my psychic ability opens up like a fan. I can hear the mountains speaking to me. I am more alive and in tune with myself than anywhere else.

Go back in your life and try to remember what movement made you feel closest to your instincts. As children, we were constantly drawn to activities in which we were able to see and hear beyond our usual range. Pretending to be a tree or a wild animal was a way to bring ourselves closer to nature, to feel in our body the same intuition we felt before we were born.

Close your eyes. Search your past for a style of movement that gives you a feeling of limitless perception. If your instincts are the sharpest when you are ice skating, carry that awareness into your walking, your driving, your dancing. It is a trick of the mind that tells us we can be psychic in only one area of our lives. If your intuition is strong when you're gardening, then your intuition can be strong on a mountain trail or in your office. Just visualize the same forces moving through your body. Slowly your instinctual responses will be distributed evenly throughout your life, and you will feel yourself in the same body everywhere you go.

Everyday Wildness

Wildness is a state of complete awareness. That's why we need it.

—GARY SNYDER

Humans are the only creatures on the planet who can disengage from the moment and lose their instincts. This can't happen to an eagle or a spider. Animals in the wild have no choice but to be bravely alive each second of the day, alert to every detail that passes through their environment. We, on the other hand, can fall into spells of anxiety, paranoia, doubt, or lose our intuition in a flood of analytical thoughts. This is good and bad at the same time. The good part is that our cerebral pathways help us write novels and build ships. The bad part is that we are able to miss out on the world around us, sacrifice a summer day worrying about our retirement.

When we invoke the warrior into our lives, our wildness stays in movement. The brain still makes its travels, but we don't lose contact with the world around us. Even though we might be musing over quantum physics or memorizing dates for history class, our body is still awake enough to sense when a car is going to slam into our lane or a butterfly cross our window. When we lived in nature, this kind of alertness was extremely important. Being able to feel a snake slithering in the grass a hundred yards away enabled you to make it back to the village in one piece. I can't help thinking how many fatal accidents could be prevented if people were just a little more present in their bodies, a little more intuitive.

Living with cats has shown me what type of psychic powers are available to us when we embrace our wildness. With their sensitive bodies, they can detect the sound of my wife's car three floors down when it enters the garage. Sometimes they even sense her arrival before she is in the neighborhood. They receive subtle transmissions that she is about to enter their habitat. They go and wait by the door, eager for the sound of her shoes on the carpet.

We, too, are capable of this kind of physical awareness. It is only our separation from nature that has thickened our skin, made us need caffeine and sugar to feel alive. Our bodies are rich with intuitive senses. The more we ignite them, the less out of place we feel in our environment.

We are not visitors to this planet. We are made from the same material as mountains and rivers. All we have to do is turn off our brains now and then and let the intelligence of the forest guide our actions. Mother Nature is always crying out for our attention. Society's addiction to violence is in some ways a call of the wild. When the animal in us isn't fed, we need to watch Rambo movies or join a gang to satisfy the craving. The trick is to find ways of being the warrior without having to carry an M16, rituals that turn on our instincts and keep us in harmony with the planet.

Only when we repress our wildness does it become unmanageable. Otherwise it is a loyal and protecting guide, like a wolf, able to lead us out of the maze and into our real lives. It is no wonder that in urban cultures so many young people feel lost and hopeless. Nature has a way of showing us what species we are, what dreams and passions lie dormant in our body. Many inner-city children never get to climb a tree. I can't think of who I would have become had I not been given all those hours in my childhood to hunt bull frogs and build forts in the bushes. It was in these moments that my soul spoke to me, that the writer and the psychic started to record life.

In order to regain your instincts, you need to revive your wildness, find ways to be as alert and present standing in line at the bank as your ancestors were stalking an elk through the forest. We can bring the wilderness back into the city by bringing the wilderness back into our bodies.

Here is an exercise I have discovered that will increase the wildness in your everyday life, and make your body more psychic. As always, if any personal ritual comes to you that I fail to mention, do it. Follow your gut. That is what this book is all about.

◉ Finding a Wild Character

It is helpful in awakening your instincts to have a character you play that is not a civilian, someone who has no concept of microwaves and traffic signs, a wild person, a creature of the forest. To invoke this character, you might dance to drums every day in your living room or go hiking with your friends in the mountains with nothing but sneakers on. The character might seduce you into going out for a rib dinner once a month and eating with your hands, or participating in Native American rain dances.

When I was growing up, the way my mother expressed her wildness was to jump on the back of her thoroughbred and go galloping through the fields. At these moments she became another woman, her hair flying in the wind like gypsy lightning, her body alive and free.

It is only an illusion that the city is less dangerous than the jungle. Just because we have escalators and indoor plumbing doesn't mean we are excluded from nature's fierceness. Look how many decisions you are asked to make in a day that require a warrior's precision and timing. Just driving your kids home from school can turn on the hunter in you, make your eyes see farther and your hearing more alert.

If you let your wild character develop, these moments of stress will be easier to tolerate. Your boss will ask you for an idea and the answer will be right inside you, without doubt, without hesitation, your body responding with its own swift intelligence. A mugger will be following you on the street and you'll know what to do to protect yourself. You won't freeze up. The warrior will guide you. Your body will stay in motion.

A lot of people think that by doing wild things you become more violent. The only time this happens is when you neglect the other parts of yourself—the lover, the mystic, the healer. The beauty of disciplines such as martial arts and fencing is that they teach you how to direct your wildness in a way that is in harmony with the soul. The Sufi dervishes were masters of this. They could take on the ferocity of the wolf and not grow fangs, or step into the fire and not be burned.

I suggest getting to know your wild character over time, rather than trying to define him or her all at once. With the New Age movement, people are a little too eager to start dressing in doeskin boots and calling themselves Soaring Hawk. Just follow your heart. Give yourself some time every few weeks to strip away your masks and mate with nature.

Maybe your first ritual will be simply to sit alone on the beach once a month and breathe in the salt air, allowing your body to remember all the past lives you spent at one with nature. Often we just have to make a subtle adjustment in an activity—wear a certain piece of clothing, carry a certain stone—to awaken its primitive underpinnings. The warrior in us can sniff out the essence of our modern habits, show us how to change our wood cutting so that it carries the same grace and feeling our ancestors expressed thousands of years ago.

My friend Lorin, who is always giving me new ideas for how to live an interesting life, suggested I meditate one day a month in a room on a bearskin rug. This might sound like a strange idea in the late twentieth century, but three hundred years ago this would have been considered a normal path to wisdom. Every indigenous culture has a way of honoring the wild, untamed side of man. Without this, we become intellectual mind-beasts, capable of sawing down forests and poisoning lakes. Get to know your wild character. See what she likes to wear and eat, what sounds she makes, how she walks, dances, sits. If you have children, they will love this. You can enter the instinctual world together.

If this ritual intimidates you, think of it as play, rather than something crazy and out of control. The wild character in us is the one who acts without thinking, who can swing from a tree, dance, bark like a dog, just for the pure fun of being alive. This is really what wildness is . . . life expressing itself. When you return to this state of being, you will realize how perceptive you are, how much psychic communication takes place in nature. Don't complicate things. The forest doesn't think so much. It just is.

I remember when I lived in Montreal I got the craving one evening to go walking through the park alone at midnight. It wasn't a very safe decision, but I was young, and logic was not my leading companion.

I will never forget what it felt like to be alone in the trees, hearing the tapping of a light rainfall on the branches. The pretense of the modern world vanished, and all that was left was nature, the ancient sounds and feelings that have touched man since the beginning of time.

I stayed in the forest for a few hours, running around, dodging bushes, leaping through the mist. I could hear voices calling me, the ancestors who still lived in these enchanted woods. My intuition became electric. I knew which path to take, what hill to climb, when to stop and wait for a sign.

I never realized before how protective nature is, how our instinct to survive is a psychic force, able to guide us through the most precarious moments. Everything that is living is guided by this power: flies, rabbits, chickens. In order to stay living, they must follow their instinctual cues with total trust, let go and surrender to the dance of creation.

When I came back to my neighborhood, I felt as if I had been out walking with God. My body was trembling with fear and joy. I saw some Orthodox Jews on my street and immediately approached them, asking if I could join them in their morning worship. They didn't feel like strangers. Their black coats and long beards seemed familiar, an image from my past.

I wonder what it would be like to live a whole life like this, to get to know nature so well that she would never leave your side; she would always be whispering things to you through the cells of your skin, leading you fearlessly into all the experiences your heart craves.

Joseph Campbell said that what is more important to humans than finding a meaning for life is to feel alive. I don't recommend going into the park alone at midnight, but do something. Allow yourself moments to forget that you are living in the twentieth century. Feel a bird's flight tugging at your skin, hear the wind as it combs the trees. It will change you. You will get a glimpse of the body you are inhabiting, how much it knows, how much it sees, how deeply it listens.

The warrior has ears for the wild, able to feel what nature is going to do next before it happens. It is said that certain fish can predict earthquakes, that horses and dogs know when a storm is coming. Let your awareness be attuned to the wilderness, to the instincts that pulse through everything that is alive.

From your head to your toes, sense the world around you right now. What is really happening? What are your instincts telling you to do?

The Edge

It is our light, not our darkness, that most frightens us.
                                          —NELSON MANDELA

 Whenever I give people a reading, I always try to uncover what their edge is, where they are afraid to walk but need to in order to stay loyal to their soul's path. It is at the edge where guidance comes to us most clearly, where our psychic ability is the strongest. For some people, going to therapy and facing their emotions is the edge. For another person, it might be spending more time with his children, or enrolling in a stand-up comedy class.

At first the edge is always uncomfortable, because it forces you to change, to walk into a new power and abandon the habits that keep you small and afraid. The more we go to this place, the stronger our instincts become. Clichés such as "Live every moment as if it were your last" or "Suck the marrow out of life" are there to encourage us to be fully alive each second we are here. For this reason, Zen appeals to me a lot. In Zen there is a way to cut a cucumber with greatness, a way to mop the floor with the same focus as a lion tamer. When we live with this kind of electric presence, following our soul with immediacy and courage, our intuition blossoms. The edge is where the voices are the loudest, where your soul doesn't need a calling card to reach you.

Have you ever noticed when you are sick how much easier it is to know what your body needs, how clear the messages are? *Eat soup. Sleep. Eat more soup. Go for a walk. Breathe.* This is the edge. All the signals are louder there. You don't need a psychic to tell you what is going on. The answer is right in your face.

Unfortunately, in our modern culture, we don't honor the edge very much. Most of us habitually push our true needs down deep inside ourselves until somewhere far into the future they explode all around us. The problem is, when you always run away from new challenges, your instincts become weak. As human beings, we need to confront our demons on a regular basis to keep our soul close to us. In other words, we need the edge to grow. Pushing ourselves beyond our limits is a way of keeping our antennae pointed in the sky, alert to all the messages the universe wants to send us.

And don't get me wrong, the edge has nothing do with being careless or taking unnecessary risks. The edge is not suicide. It is more about freedom and joy, about allowing yourself to act from a place of intuition at the expense of your fears.

Gandhi once said that living nonviolently means that if you see someone being mugged on the street, you will go and risk your life to save him. This is the edge. It is full of heart and compassion, because it is love in action. There are no theories on the edge. This is the place where the dove is set free from your hand, where the smoke changes directions, where the violin begins to play and the body follows.

Where in modern society do we have a place to train ourselves to live in this bold frequency? Most schools are definitely not a training ground for the spiritual warrior. There are so many rules set up in most institutions, that an act of heart, of brave originality, is often criticized or punished. In order to learn how to live on the edge, with light in our step, requires that we build our own temples, our own sacred environment, where we can behave without restraint and not be judged.

For some people, this might mean taking a dance class once a week or building an art studio at the back of their house. In whatever way you can make space in your life for more intensity, more passion, the warrior in you will flourish.

The night I began writing this chapter was definitely a night of living on the edge. Every reading I gave demanded a level of honesty that four years ago I would have been afraid to express.

In many of the readings the messages I gave to my clients were uncomplicated and direct. To one girl I said, "You have a very brave heart." This one sentence created a stillness between us as deep as a canyon. We looked at each other closely. It was near the end of the reading. Nothing more needed to be said.

I learned that night that at the edge things get really simple. When your body is acting from an instinctual place, the choices are few. Your soul gives you a cue and you follow it. It will warn you against danger or lead you to the right place at the right time. The more familiar you are with living this way, the less you have to think.

The Chinese have an expression, "What today is a blade of grass, tomorrow is a tree." When we follow the warrior along the blade of the moment, we attend to our problems the moment they need to be taken care of. Nothing is left undone. Whatever needs to be accomplished happens effortlessly, in the right time. When we move forward, the path behind us is filled with light.

Some dancers are masters at edge walking. Each step is so precise, so fluid, that the path they create cuts through time and exposes the infinite. I believe the universe was created this efficiently, with thin grooves of light we all must follow, that lead us deeper and deeper into ourselves, until eventually we are no longer trapped in any one place, able to soar through all of creation. The Buddha achieved this. After sitting under the Bodhi tree and facing all his fears, he could walk anywhere. The universe was for his choosing. He became an instrument in a great song.

Once a week I host a poetry reading in Hollywood. People come from all over town to share their verse. At the end of each night we play an improv game I invented called Zen poetry. The game involves finding words in yourself without rehearsal, walking a verbal tightrope from one place to another with just the velocity of your own soul. This type of poetry activates the same voice that one uses in a psychic reading. It's a fantastic exercise, drawing out of people jewels they would never have found had they been following their logical mind.

At one of my readings a young Asian man came in who was a beginner poet. He read some of his poems and they were pretty good. When it came around to Zen poetry time, he eagerly went up to the mike and dropped a few words. By far, it was the best poem of the night. I can't remember it in total detail, but he said something like this.

When you are walking though your life and searching for answers, sometimes you come upon a large urn, an ancient shape in the mud that stirs something in you so deep, that it starts to change your life the moment you touch it. It is hard to describe the urn, because it is so beautiful, because it fits so well in your hands. You never thought that you would find something like this, and now you have. It's right in front of you, alive and moving . . .

As he was speaking, his eyes were closed. His body was trembling. He was standing on the edge. He was giving the whole room a poem, a psychic message we could all take home with us and apply in our life.

For each of us, the urn meant something different. For me, it meant honesty, living so true in each moment, that there is no regret, no guilt, no wasted time. We don't have forever in this body. We have a small slice of eternity in which to find our gifts and share them with the world. Living on the edge means that you face your fears consistently until they no longer rule you. The less afraid we are, the more the warrior can guide us, giving our body psychic cues exactly when we need them.

For many of us, it takes the presence of death to wake us up to this awareness—cancer, jail, the loss of a loved one. Start now. Bring the edge into your life so that you don't need to create one of these hard lessons to wake yourself up. If you act ahead of time, you can dodge some of the punches, create a life with more joy and less struggle.

Leonard Cohen has a line that I say when I am standing on the edge, when the walls are melting and the fire is rising around my heart. "Dance me through the panic till I'm gathered safely in." These are the words I chant when I'm on the edge. And the gates of heaven always open.

◎ Soul Callings and Dares

A calling of the soul is an opportunity to expand and fulfill your deepest potential. It is usually a heightened experience which opens your heart, and it can also shake you to the core. How long you shake depends on how much shaking you need. Some of us have a lot of dead leaves on our branches and need a good storm in order to meet spring again. A dare, on the other hand, is a form of self-sabotage, an invitation to be led into unnecessary danger. Learning the difference between a calling of the soul and a dare can save your life.

Getting on your Harley-Davidson and rushing through downtown traffic at ninety miles an hour is a dare. Standing up at Carnegie Hall in front of two thousand people and singing your guts out is a calling of the soul. So is leading an old person across the street, or standing up for yourself against an abusive friend. These both fall into the second, more luminous category.

The warrior is not stupid, says my friend who is a black belt in Kempo Karate. He knows when to act, when to draw his sword and slay the dragon, and when to wait. In a dare, we can get crushed, because the universe is not supporting us. When we follow our soul's calling, however, we find grace. We grow wings rather than claws. Something carries us, lifts us through the storm and into safety.

Being in a body means that each of us has chosen to walk the edge, to enter into the unknown and seek out the light. To keep this walk swift and graceful, we need to respond to as many of our soul callings as possible. Sometimes they are big and sometimes they are small. Some evenings just to brush my teeth before going to bed is walking the edge. I have a habit of being the absentminded poet, writing until four in the morning and then just collapsing on the couch.

Be present for what your edge is every moment. Learn the difference between caring for yourself and pampering your fears. Write a list of all the actions you want to take in your life that challenge you. Figure out which are dares and which are callings of the soul. Erase the dares. You don't need them. They are a waste of energy. Now go out and do the rest. Put each calling into movement.

I will tell you right now what my soul callings are, what psychic guidance my soul is handing me this second.

1. Memorize a Psalm from the Bible for strength.
2. Teach lots of workshops and be a playful magician in the moment with no fear and lots of surprises.

3. Find a place to connect with old people, maybe in a retirement home, to feed and be fed.
4. Be still and wait for guidance rather than inventing maps that aren't real.
5. Teach with words that are in harmony with the blood that runs through all human beings.
6. Cherish the innocent child and do things for him that are simple and clean.
7. Read library books about everything.
8. Don't forget love, everywhere, always, forever.

Make a promise to yourself that you will write down each month what your soul callings are, and in the following month, put some of them into action. It is likely that many of the soul callings you have will take years to fulfill, and others will happen in a jiffy.

The moment you identify what your soul callings are, you will start to change. For example, if you make the decision today to become a doctor, right away your body will start to take on the characteristics you need to walk that road. Intuitively, you will be led to the right people, the right schools, the right books. The more you honor your soul callings, the more psychic you will become. You will start to know which events and people in your life are supporting your destiny and which ones are leading you astray.

Identifying what you are here to do allows the world to help you achieve your goals. But remember one thing: If it is your calling to be a doctor, it might not be the type of doctor you think. Your soul might want you as an acupuncturist rather than a surgeon. Just because the door looks one way from the outside doesn't mean the room behind it is the same.

The universe is always improving itself. Some of our ideas of the future are medieval compared to what is really going to happen. We always have to be prepared for something a little more advanced and state of the art. Just as technology is rapidly changing, so is our destiny. New scenes are being added each moment, new degrees of consciousness. If we open ourselves and trust the leadership of our soul, the path we are on can shift into something even more beautiful than we ever imagined. This is the miracle of living on the edge: the grass is always greener than you expected.

Another thing you can do is to make a collage. You can cut out pictures and words from magazines that resonate with your soul callings, and pin them artistically on a piece of cardboard in your bedroom. This will keep you awake to your purpose every morning as you wake up, get the warrior humming through your cells before you even eat breakfast.

Remember, we are wild creatures. We are here to make the impossible possible. Find yourself some heroes who fulfilled soul callings that are similar to yours. Read about them and see what they did to overcome the obstacles that stand in your way. As Joseph Campbell said, the labyrinth has been walked a thousand times. We are not alone in life. With each step, we meet others who have taken a similar journey. The great ones are with us all the way.

FIVE MORE WAYS TO SUMMON THE WARRIOR

1. Practice silence. Whether it be with your lover, your friend, or your pet, learn how to be wordless and communicate through the eyes, gestures, and subtle vibration. Go on a silent two-hour hike or cook and eat dinner with someone without saying a thing. This will awaken your instincts, make you more telepathic and intuitive with everything around you.

2. Learn how to sense objects and people in your environment through your body. When you come home at night, close your eyes and perceive everything around you through the sensors on your skin. Feel the chairs and tables as energy rather than solid matter, and determine what the personality of each piece of furniture is, how it makes you feel. When you sit beside someone, let your body tell you who she is. Trust your instincts. The body knows things on its own. It doesn't need proof. It goes right to the source.

3. Attempt a sport like archery or karate, which requires an intimate connection between mind, body, and spirit. Bring this awareness into your daily life. Be precise and focused in your actions, always aware of your breath, your intention, and your surroundings. Be like Robin Hood. Split the arrows on the bull's-eye. Go right for the mark.

4. Go to the zoo and study the animals. Find out which ones

you relate to and why. Discover ways to activate their awareness in your body, ways that are subtle and discreet. My favorite animals to watch are orangutans. They are real masters. They know how to just sit and be. They love to observe life, to observe all the details of your character as if you were from another world. I have found ways to imitate them with my breath and posture. They have taught me a lot.

Warning: Don't come to work screeching like a bat. Make the exercise more internal. Not everyone will understand what you are doing.

5. Be more aware of smell. When you are with people, take in their scent. You can tell a lot about someone through your nose. Smell is an instinctual sense; it never lies. Smell the world everywhere you go, and find out what smells you like the best. During her speech at a writer's conference, a woman told the audience that she goes out with her dog every night into the field to smell. She can now detect what animals are on her property—badgers, foxes, coyotes. Our noses can be strong if we want them to be. Just smell and smell, and your instincts will get more refined.

PART V

Invoking the Shaman

Guides

The most beautiful thing we can experience is the mysterious.

—ALBERT EINSTEIN

 We all have guides. There are spirits who walk with us our entire lives that live behind the veil on the other side of time. Before we are born, they agree to join us in our travels, to assist us in carrying out the challenges of our soul's path. Usually we have known our guides before in past lives. They are like old friends, companions from a long voyage. When we meet them again after death, we will recognize their presence, and remember all the times they served us as we stumbled through the world.

The more in sync you are with your guides, the easier it is to follow your intuition, to have contact with other dimensions. Guides are messengers, couriers of spiritual ideas. When we are open to their wisdom, we take on a shamanistic role. We can draw into our life information that has a profound impact on the world around us, healing ourselves and others in ways we never thought possible.

Many artists refer to their guides as muses, invisible spirits that help them create compelling art. Other people refer to their guides as guardian angels or divine protectors. How you name these forces doesn't matter. You could be a total atheist and they will still stand by you in difficult times. Guides are loyal and have great compassion for the human experience. They know how easy it is for us to forget about the other world. They don't take it personally.

Sometimes our relatives and loved ones turn into guides the moment they die. Out of their love for us, they choose to stay behind until we finish our term, or pass through a critical trial. At certain moments we might feel them in the room with us, floating over our shoulder giving us advice. Other times we might hear them in our mind, telling us the same joke they told us a hundred times before, lightening our load, giving us encouragement and support.

There are a myriad of ways our guides communicate with us: telepathy, clairvoyance, dreams. Much of their guidance slips past our rational mind. We find ourselves changing lanes for no reason at all, purchasing a book we never thought we'd buy, taking an unexpected trip. Our guides help us stay on track with all the things we are here to accomplish, be still when we need to, or act when the timing is right.

Not all of us are meant to have visual contact with our guides. Some of us are here on missions of faith that require we give up certain soul powers and move through life by feeling alone. Other people are born with more refined senses, able to see and hear their guides from the time they are children. Maria Altea, the author of *The Eagle and the Rose,* is such a person. She interacts with the spirit world like a journalist, able to send and receive visionary images with the clarity of a television set.

Where you fall on the spectrum doesn't matter. Even if you have never seen or heard your guides, this doesn't mean they aren't active in your life. A tree doesn't have to have eyes to be nourished by the sun. Your guides are with you no matter what. They are woven into your experience like a constellation of stars. Your ambitions, your dreams, your desires are as important to them as they are to you. When you accept this, and allow your guides to have a stronger presence in your life, everything you do will be enhanced. Your creativity will flourish; your job will be smoother; your relationships will have more depth.

My mother's guides help her find parking spaces on crowded weekends, direct her to garage sales, give her solace in lonely times. Your guides can assist you in everything from the mundane to the sacred. All they need is a place in your heart, an agreement that you embrace their support. My sister says her guides always tell her not to take things too seriously. They add a playful dimension to her life, keeping her laughing on dark days. My guides give me a feeling of protection. They bring me back to reality when my mind is running out on the perimeter, when a psychic reading has taken me deep into the forest and I need a road home.

How your guides interact with you depends on the challenges you are facing. If you have cancer, your guides can help you heal your body, directing you to the right doctors and healers to strengthen your immune system. If you are in jail, your guides can ease your loneliness, giving you deeper insight into your problems so that you may walk into the world a wiser person.

Whatever it is that you have come up against—illness, heart-break, depression—your guides can show you how to work through the pain and create a happier life. All you have to do is ask and believe, and then let things take their course. With your permission, your guides can work faster and with more efficiency. To give our guides free rein to serve us, we need to give them the go-ahead, to open the hangar and let the jets roar into the sky.

At the end of this chapter, I will teach you a ritual you can perform to have more intimacy with your guides. Do it when you feel ready to move into deeper union with your soul. There is no rush. Your guides are with you right now. Before you call them, they are already in your presence. Before you dial their number, they've already picked up the phone.

◎ Preparing the Body

Since our guides live at a more refined frequency than we do, to be in close contact with them can sometimes stimulate a lot of emotion in our bodies, bringing to the surface everything in us that needs to be healed. For this reason, we can experience a rush of painful memories when they come close to us, because their mere presence is able to cure our bodies.

If you grew up in a household with a lot of trauma, when you communicate with your guides, sometimes your body will go through a quick discharge of panic. Your heart will beat faster. You will feel scared and alone just as you did when you were young. Then after a few long minutes, the relaxation will hit. You will cross a threshold and everything will be calm and soothing again.

If you are not carrying a lot of trauma in your body, then

communing with your guides will not bring about any intense side effects. You will simply feel that your energy has been elevated, that you are in a lighter world, with fewer barriers between you and your soul.

Moving closer to the spirit world is like deep-sea diving. You have to go through different phases of growth so that you can endure the depths and intensity of spiritual contact. Healing the emotional pain stored in your body is the best preparation you can give yourself. Not only will it help you become more psychic, it will also carve a pathway between you and your guides, so that they can have a deeper influence in your life.

Therapy, massage, acupuncture, Reiki, and meditation have all played a part in my healing. Follow your intuition. Perform the activities that are calling you. Sometimes just a walk in the park is a starting point, or reading a good book. Ask your soul for guidance. Healing is the one thing that cannot wait. We all must begin our work today.

◎ The Circle

In moments of need, our guides surround us in a circle and feed us messages from each side of our body like a wheel of light. As we are out walking in the evening, they might give us the impulse to take another route home so that we avoid danger. At a party, they might lead us to speak with a stranger who just happens to be married to one of our old friends. When our guides influence us like this, we become part of a collaborative event, a composition of movement that ripples out into the world like music, adding soul exactly where it is needed.

You can practice cultivating these moments at home by meditating on the presence of your guides standing around you in a circle. Doing a ritual like this every week will keep you more attuned to the guidance they are offering you moment to moment as you move through the world.

I suggest trying this next exercise with a couple of close friends as well. The shaman part of us is amplified in the presence of those we love. When two or more come together, the dynamic expands.

Here's how the ritual works.

Once or twice a week, sit in a chair in the center of the most peaceful room in your house and meditate on a memory in which you felt guided and cared for. It could be anything—the time you gave an enlightened speech, experienced a close call on the freeway, caught a pop fly in the last inning of a baseball game . . . whatever you want. Bring the memory into your body and sit with it until it fills you to the brim.

Then when you are ready, visualize a ray of light pouring out of the top of your head in multiple directions like the spokes of a wheel. Imagine at the end of each spoke a guide standing and watching you, someone who loves and understands your soul.

In your mind's eye, count how many guides you see and what each of them looks like. Get acquainted with how it feels to have them around you, the safety of their presence.

At first you might not feel anything. Don't worry about it. It takes time for your senses to become open enough to detect subtle vibrations. Each time you do the exercise, you will feel your guides with a greater sensitivity. It will happen gradually, over time.

Try this exercise also when you are in a creative moment, such as writing a story, acting, or giving a sermon at church; or feel your guides around you in a circle when you are out walking in the neighborhood or planting flowers in your garden.

The more you call on your guides, the more involved they will be in your life. Once you establish a connection with them, talk with them as you would talk to a close friend. Use mental telepathy to invoke their presence everywhere you go. Remember, they are your support system, there to help you as you journey through the world.

As I was writing this chapter, I felt my guides surrounding my chair, sending me quiet inspiration: an old man, a young woman, and a child. The old man encourages me to have faith and to love myself. The young woman is a messenger of freedom and joy. And the child is there to remind me to trust no matter how scary things get. How many guides are with you? What are their names? What do they have to tell you?

This ritual will help you establish a meeting point between you and your guides, but the meeting itself will happen only when the time is right, when you are ready to encounter the further dimensions of your soul.

It is possible that you have only one guide, that there is not a circle of spirits around you, but only one. Quantity doesn't matter. Being aware of a single guide is a treasure. Take what you find and honor it. It is a blessing to have contact with the other side. It is the beginning of the long road home.

Everything in life can be our guide if we allow it—a bird, a leaf, a stranger we meet on the bus. The whole universe is evolving back into light, back into pure space. When you are open to your guides, it is easier to stay in tune with this river of change, to participate in life in a way that benefits the whole.

I always think of my guides as musicians, wise souls who have learned how to create harmony through the chaos of existence. They have always been there for me. The older I get, the more I feel them in my heart. I have a feeling that by the time I am an old man, I will see them as I see my wife, vivid, pulsating, alive. For now they are only visible in my mind's eye, too subtle a vibration for the material plane.

Let your guides slowly come into your life, one whisper at a time. You will stop feeling so alone. Your heart will open. You will make it through the difficult moments with less struggle.

Ask for their love and support and see what happens. If you can't believe in such a thing as a guide, ask the child inside you to help you believe. As children, we were open to magic. If a butterfly could exist, so could an angel. It made sense. Life was a miracle. Anything was possible.

Rituals

Learning is movement from moment to moment.
—J. KRISHNAMURTI

 Rituals are like bells. They bring you into the moment. They reduce the stress in your body and push you into deeper contact with your soul. Whatever you need to hear, whatever intuitive messages are tugging at your sleeve, become clear and audible. The horns may still be honking, the subway still pulsing through the ground, but your channels are open. There is a space of listening inside you. You are awake and receptive.

Even though it can be a daily practice, ritual is the opposite of routine. In a ritual, the clock stops ticking. Your shaman self is unveiled, and you enter what the Aborigines call the dreamtime. A simple act, such as lighting a candle or tapping a stick on the ground, is suddenly full of magic and meaning. You are no longer just a machine fulfilling a task. Your body is connected to the earth, the stars, the rug beneath your feet. Each breath is important, each movement an invocation of the gods.

Any activity that brings harmony to your senses, relaxes you, makes the ordinary sacred, carries a force of ritual. Writing in your journal is a ritual. Painting is a ritual. Saying a prayer before you eat is a ritual. A ritual is not so much what you do as how you do it. Walking through the park could be a ritual, or going to a café and drinking tea. The only difference between a ritual and a normal event is your state of mind. When you are in a ritual, you can't be anywhere else. You are completely connected to the action you are performing. There is no space to worry about bills or next year's Christmas list. If you are drinking tea, then that is all you are doing. Otherwise you lose your concentration and your intuition diminishes.

Rituals help us move in the world with greater instinct and timing. They teach us how to be totally present in the moment, able to carry out actions with a clear and focused mind. The ancient Samurai of Japan used ritual in this manner, as a way to sharpen their awareness for the crucible of battle. When they spent hours polishing their armor, it was not an act of vanity, but rather an exercise that trained them to live with heightened attention. Being able to make a sword shine like the sun meant that you were able to give all of yourself to a single purpose, and thus invoke your soul in whatever you were doing.

One of my daily rituals is walking. When it feels like the right time, I just leave my apartment and cruise around the neighborhood for a while. Rather than trying to invoke psychic messages, I just let my mind go blank and place my attention on all the details around me: street signs, trees, children riding bicycles. I trust that if there is something I am meant to hear, the information will just rise up on its own. I don't need to force it. Just being in a ritual atmosphere is enough. As long as I am open and alert, then I will be able to receive whatever wants to come to me.

When I went for a walk last night, about three blocks into my travels, the rest of this chapter appeared in my mind. I was not thinking about it. It just floated up like a treasure, arriving in my head with perfect clarity. This is the magic of ritual. You plan to do a simple thing with all of your attention, and something more happens: insights, discoveries, predictions. Whatever you need to see or hear is made available to you, because you have created a space where your soul may communicate with you.

The more intense and demanding your life is, the more ritual you need. If your job is gardening, and you spend eight hours a day watering plants and nursing trees, then you might not require the same degree of ritual as if you manage a company or have five children. It is quite easy to be in tune with yourself when you are cutting roses or planting bulbs in the earth. This is a ritual in itself.

But when you are locked in an office, with faxes humming and phones ringing, you need to schedule rituals for yourself that take you out of the madness and into a more psychic state of mind.

In the old days, ritual was more a part of everyday life. Nature herself would draw us into moments of deep listening. We would be called to stop our wood chopping for a few minutes and go and sit by the river. At this time our bodies would tell us that a storm was on its way, or that we were going to have a new child, or what animal we should hunt for dinner.

Ritual diminishes when as a society we stop honoring our existence. As Westerners, we get moving so fast that we lose track of how miraculous our lives are and, in turn, stop giving ourselves the time we need to reflect and gather ourselves. When this happens, our psychic ability weakens. We start to run on autopilot, making the same mistakes over and over again, rather than stopping every so often to check inside and see what guidance our soul is offering us.

There are subtle rhythms in the body which, if we follow them, refine our psychic ability and make us more alert to what we need to do moment to moment to stay healthy and growing. In the wilderness, these rhythms are easier to follow, because everything around us is already obeying these principles. But in civilization, we have to create our own internal clocks. Sometimes just a five-minute ritual every two hours can minimize stress and keep the intuitive channels open.

◎ Creating Daily Rituals

For most of us, our daily rituals are centered on our bodies. Many of us aren't very comfortable in our skin, so we do things at regular intervals to ease the pain: smoke pot, munch chocolate bars, drink beer, watch videos. These types of rituals are fine now and then, but in excess, they tend to stifle our instincts, make us feel numb and lost. When you create daily rituals, you need to find things that relax you, but at the same time wake you up. The more you equate peace with alertness, the more psychic you will become.

To begin with, do a mental tracking of your day. List all the rituals you do and put a check mark beside the ones that feed your soul, and an X beside the rituals you feel you have outgrown, that are somehow getting in the way of your soul's path. Remember, a ritual can be anything: watching TV, walking, meditating, painting, writing. A lot of the rituals we do are so blended into our life that we forget they are rituals. Study yourself closely. See what rituals you have formed and why you do them.

When you are ready, examine your list. Ask yourself what is missing, what rituals from this book you could perform that would help you stay more in league with your intuition, and at what times of the day they should happen.

I have a much better sense of ritual at night than I do in the morning. After the sun sinks down, I am as methodical as a brain surgeon. I am in a state of deep listening, alive to all the signals I need to hear. But in the morning I am a sloth. Sometimes the only ritual I can put together is to go down to the gas station and buy a coffee. Consequently, in the morning I am not as psychic. My instincts are duller, because my sense of ritual is not as developed.

For some people having a beer every day after work might be a fine ritual. It could be relaxing, even meditative. But for another person it might be a mode of escape, a retreat into oblivion. Really look hard at yourself and see what rituals stifle you and which ones open you up to an intuitive and creative frame of mind.

Remember, sometimes just a slight modification can turn an ordinary habit into a ritual. For instance, if you have a nightly news habit, try doing some yoga as you watch. It might influence you to assimilate the information on a more intuitive level, one that causes you less stress and more relaxation. Often we don't need to throw away the activities we have chosen in our life; we just need to reshape them, give them new intentions that feed our soul.

As I tell my students, if you dislike your job, figure out what rituals you can do each day to make the commitment more bearable. Start with simple things and work your way up. If you are working in an office, make the decision before work to take a small walk or meditate for ten minutes before you eat lunch. Maybe there is a bookstore nearby that has a volume of poetry you like. Go there every lunch hour and randomly select a poem to read, then carry the feeling of the poem back into your afternoon as a kind of magical talisman.

Rituals develop slowly over time. Don't be in a rush. Just start with a few basic activities and let it snowball into a way of life. Before you know it, you will be just as psychic behind the stove as you are with your prayer beads and a stick of incense.

In the next section, I am going to explain briefly how you can use the four elements—earth, air, water, and fire—in your rituals, and how each of them will affect your psychic development. The shamans of old relied on the balance of these elements to make their flight into the dream world stable and secure.

Remember, ritual and play are not that far apart. Sometimes building a sand castle can be the most ritualistic thing we do. I have had many psychic revelations while in a moment of sacred play. Enjoy yourself. Be creative. If you get the urge to finger-paint every morning before work, do so. Follow your impulses. They will lead you somewhere, somewhere close to your soul.

◎ Fire

By awakening your psychic ability, you are initiating yourself into deeper union with your soul. If you are at the beginning of this path, fire is the element to focus on. Fire makes you more alert. It awakens your primitive mind and allows you to experience the world more through sensing than reason.

A great way to include fire in a ritual is to light a tall candle and spend ten or twenty minutes meditating on it every day for a week. While you are staring at the flame, imagine the fire entering into your body through your eyes and filling you slowly all the way down to your feet. If you do this exercise consistently, it will help you dissolve the mental barriers that prevent you from connecting with your intuition and awaken you more to your soul's path.

In the presence of fire, whatever messages are stirring inside us become easier to interpret and speak. We become poets, storytellers, magicians, able to communicate from the heart with less awkwardness and fear.

When we focus on the fire element, we draw into the body a force of change and purification. When we are at a crossroads in life, being molded into a new shape, we are in a sense "on fire." If for most of your life you have lived in a rational, concrete world, far from your instincts, try performing some rituals with fire every day to awaken new senses. The ritual could be as simple as lighting incense and praying for ten minutes, or as wild as doing a fire dance with friends in the woods.

Last year on a camping trip with my wife, we lit a huge fire and performed a ritual in which we each threw an article into the flames that we felt was holding us back from living our soul's path. I threw in a book written by my favorite author in an attempt to find more of my own voice and writing style. My wife threw in a brand new tablecloth which symbolized her desire to let go of her need for perfection.

You can use fire in whatever way you want. The rituals that come to you instinctually will have the deepest effect. Let the fire instruct you, to show you what needs to be done to invoke your psychic talents. Be willing to experiment. If some sort of chant comes into you as you are sitting in front of your candle, then say it. Let heaven speak through you the way it did to the healers and psychics of the past. This is the path of the shaman.

◎ Water

Shamans have been using water in rituals for thousands of years. Water purifies the body, prepares it for sacred ceremony. Water helps you wipe away the static in your magnetic field so that your perceptions are clearer. As babies, our first nine months were spent in water. Whenever we return to a liquid environment, the cells in our body relax. We connect with the force that guided us into this world, the primordial feminine energy we knew as our mother.

Since our bodies are ninety-six percent water, it is important we stay in tune with this element. We need to have the relationship with water that we experienced as children, playing in it, resting in it, using it to wash away our worries and fears.

A wonderful way to use water in a ritual is to dip your hands in a bowl of it while you meditate. This will awaken the intuitive channels in your body and connect you with your deeper emotions. It is also good to add some salt to your bowl of water to give it the qualities of the sea. If you repeat a meditation like this a few times a month, you will find that you are much more relaxed and in tune with your instincts. When a problem arises, the spirit of water will be in your consciousness. You will be more yielding, and more open to divine guidance.

When I am in the midst of a good reading, my body feels like a river. The words rise out of me with an effortless flow. I can feel the presence of other beings moving around me like large underwater mammals. I feel protected, safe, guided.

When we leave this planet, we will enter an ocean much like

the one we see when we are standing on the beach. There will be fewer boundaries between ourselves and others. Learning to exist with this feeling of closeness while we are still in a body is what water teaches us. To be psychic means to be intimate with life, to know others as we know ourselves. Whenever you want to feel less isolated, more at one with your soul, go to the water. Run a bath, go swimming, dance in the rain. Let water encompass you, suffuse the dry thirsty corners of your body and bring you home.

⊚ Earth

The more you develop your psychic ability, the more you need to connect with the earth to keep you grounded. Without the earth beneath our feet, we blow away like a kite with a broken string. While we are on the planet, we need the earth to give us roots, foundation, gravity.

In the final moment of temptation with Kamasara, the Lord of Darkness, Buddha touched the earth with his left hand to confirm that he still knew what was real. This is the power of earth. When we are swept away by delusions and fantasies, earth takes the wind out of our sails. It gives us the stable presence we need to balance our minds and attend to our intuition.

There are many ways you can use earth in your rituals to keep yourself centered and focused. One of my favorites is sculpting clay. Anytime you are feeling disconnected from your body and your instincts, go to the art store and purchase a large piece of clay. Bring it home and place it on a piece of plastic in the center of your living room. Close your eyes. Begin to touch and mold the clay by pure feeling alone. Don't worry about aesthetics. Sculpt an image that reflects the natural beauty of your soul. This exercise will ground you in the body, and give you the stability and confidence you need to carry out your soul's path.

Working in the garden planting flowers and vegetables is another way to commune with the earth. A friend of mine told me she can hear her bulbs singing in the spring when the sun heats up. Being a gardener has enhanced her intuition, made her more in tune with the cycles of growth natural to all living things.

Also, doing simple rituals like walking on the beach, hiking, or playing golf, will keep your psychic ability rooted in the ground. You will grow wings, but not lose your footing. If you are one of those people who is easily spaced out, try spending time around large animals such as horses and cows. Petting their bodies and watching them move will serve as an antidote for unwarranted space travel.

Earth reminds us to go slowly, that everything strong and enduring takes a long time to develop. I include earth in my rituals all the time. When I am hiking in the mountains, I hug trees. When I am walking through the city, I imagine chords of energy from the earth keeping me balanced between the ground and the sky. Our roots must be as strong as our antennae. Being psychic means having a strong awareness in all directions. For the time that we are in a body, the earth is our home. The more we honor it, the more it helps us stay focused on our soul's path.

◎ Air

Air constitutes the last stage of psychic development, the final rung of the ladder. Air represents the invisible, the cosmic, the supernatural. When you begin to see and hear the other world, you are no longer trapped in one dimension. You become a switchboard for different frequencies, an oracle for traveling souls.

We encounter the element of air each time we have a thought. Air moves quickly and has no ground. It is up to us to determine which of our thoughts are real and which of our thoughts are illusory. The more connected we are to our instincts, the more discriminating we can be with our mystical experiences. We won't just believe every spiritual book we read. We will check our own internal resources, see which ideas ring true and which ones don't.

The way to use air in a ritual is to give over to spontaneous impulses, to move with the same speed as your thoughts, make up stories, perform skits with your friends, walk through a new city without a guide. Air means letting go of control, plans, agendas. People who need to do rituals with air are those who don't feel safe unless everything is mapped out. If you are afraid of the unexpected, then it is important you conduct rituals with air as your primary element, that you learn how to improvise rather than always follow a charted course. The psychic part of us flourishes when we are able to move without rehearsal, to say and do things that just pop into our mind out of nowhere like a magic trick or a bird on the windowsill.

A fantastic way to use air in a ritual is to have a spontaneous poetry gathering. Get together with one or more people and sit in a circle in one of the rooms of your house. Take turns making up poems. They could be about anything: the paintings on the wall, private emotions, famous people, colors. Speak the poems out loud to one another without stopping to think. Doing this will stimulate your psychic mind and get you communicating from a deeper place in your soul. It will create a network of energy that will open the door to hidden perceptions and feelings. The shamans of old were all spontaneous poets. Many of their cures and prayers were made up on the spot, inspired by higher forces. Doing this ritual will connect you with the magic of air, forcing you to draw on powers that dwell within.

Air is also about humor. The more air we have in us, the more we laugh. If you invent rituals that can bring you joy as much as insight, then your spirituality will never grow somber. Your intuition will always have a playful tone, a whimsical flavor.

The sprites and fairies of the forest are air creatures. They move about like pulses of sunlight, always an inch out of reach from heavy thinkers. When you let air into your being, you start to sense these subtle travelers; they are there for you when you need them, like a muse, ready to inject into your mind a quick intuitive idea to keep you on your course.

We should not try to pursue air like a drug, a fix of stardust, but rather let it emerge out of our love. When your rituals with the air element are in tune with your heart, then your spirit follows. When you get your act together on the ground, then the flying happens on its own.

Don't be surprised if your rituals start to change you, make you happier, quicker on your feet. The more you live by your own internal rhythms, the more sensitive you will become to what truly pleases you. You will know when a situation feels right, whether or not it conflicts with your nature or serves your growth.

In the colors and styles of rituals you are drawn to, you will be able to identify what past lives you have lived, what power and wisdom lies buried in your heart. From examining my own rituals, I see a deep connection with the Far East. I know I have lived there before, wandered around with a stick in my hand reciting old prayers.

Where do you come from? What rituals live in your body? Search them out. I have just given you clues, pointers. Putting them together is up to you. When you get stuck, just close you eyes and wait for a signal. There is no rush. Even if you find just one little ritualistic step each day, by the end of a year you will have created a new way of life.

Symbols

As the plant produces its flower, so does the psyche create its symbols.

—CARL JUNG

 Much of the information we receive from our intuition comes to us in the form of symbols. The soul is ancient and often does not address us in a modern, everyday language. Rather it speaks to us symbolically, using primordial images that have been floating through our brains since the beginning of time.

Symbols are rich in data. They can be read like a book, with many layers of insight to draw from. In early Egyptian times, when people of high spiritual rank gave a speech, instead of choosing a topic and following it from beginning to end, they would lift a symbol into the air and let the wisdom stored in the symbol lead them on a spiraling dialogue. The crowd participated as well. They, too, would fall into the mystery of the image, and be guided on a course of private intuitive knowledge. The Egyptians trusted that whatever needed to be spoken that day would appear on its own, summoned into the air by the magic of the symbol.

From doing years of Tarot readings, I have come to understand how it feels to be guided by symbols like this. When I am bent over the cards giving a reading, I am taken on a shamanic journey, a flight of information stimulated by these luminous shapes. Many of the things I say I have never even thought of before. The symbols in the cards invoke their own story, teaching me about my client's soul in the moment I am speaking.

At some time or another, we've all had this experience. In the right moment, almost anything can have symbolic significance and push you into an altered state of awareness. A painting on the wall could symbolically influence the poem you are writing, giving it more depth and passion. An eagle sitting on a telephone pole could expand your awareness, giving you a moment of elevated thought.

Carl Jung said that there are basically two types of symbols, those that affect us personally, such as our wife's perfume bottle or a tree from our childhood, and symbols that have a universal impact, such as a crucifix or a laughing Buddha.

In developing your psychic ability, you will come across both types of symbols. They will rise into your awareness separately and together. For example, if you ask your soul a question about your mother's health, you might receive the image of a brass bed and the Star of David. The bed is obviously a personal symbol, and the Star of David, as you know, has been around for a long time. If you examine both symbols together, there will be a link, a parallel meaning that helps you answer your question.

Interpreting symbols can sometimes be tricky because no symbol can be pinned down into a single definition. Every symbol is an encyclopedia of knowledge that you could probe and investigate your entire life. The swastika, for instance, was present in many cultures before it was appropriated by the Nazis. It was not invented by Hitler. It had been residing in the collective unconscious for thousands of years, showing up in ceremonial rites in such faraway places as Egypt and India.

Symbols are vast. They are the meeting place between body and spirit. Words from the soul often burn up when they enter the atmosphere of the mind, and come out as gibberish, but symbols are durable, like a space capsule, able to traverse multiple dimensions and stay solidly intact.

Often when a culture dies, all that's left behind are the symbols they used to define their existence. From these remains a lot can be told. Symbols reveal a people's deepest beliefs, the very foundation upon which they base their lives. I am sure when future historians look back on the evolution of Western culture and see a crucifix looming in the distance, they will know a great deal about our struggles, the path of action we took to build our world.

Before we move on, close your eyes and ask yourself what symbols have been guiding you in this life, which ones represent your deepest character. When we get in touch with the symbols of our life, we learn more about our soul's path, why we are here on the planet. The symbols I have uncovered for my own life are a sword and a heart. The sword represents communication—speaking and writing in a way that cuts through illusion and exposes truth—and the heart represents love, my guide, my teacher, my destiny.

Close your eyes and think about your symbols. If you don't have any, ask for some. Inform your soul that you would like a picture or image that is symbolic of your life. When you have something, paint it or draw it in your journal. It will be very empowering for you to know what symbols are active in your consciousness. When you feel lost or broken, you will be able to turn to these images to console you, to give you the strength to carry on.

Don't judge what symbols come to you. If you are a large muscular man and receive the symbol of a lily pad, take it in, investigate it, feel what it means to you. Often we are much different on the inside from what we are on the outside. The symbols you find will reflect your essence, the part of you only few people see.

◎ Symbols versus Psychic Visions

Telling the difference between a symbol and a psychic vision is sometimes difficult. Even after doing years of readings I still make mistakes. I can see a sailboat in my head and tell my client they are going to go sailing, when really the sailboat is symbolic of a new speed and grace in their life that has nothing to do with sailing at all.

Usually the way I separate the two is through feeling and observation. When a symbol comes into my awareness, it generally appears more like art than reality. I feel as though I am witnessing something whose meaning needs to be interpreted. And when I see a vision, I have the sense that an actual event is being revealed before my eyes. Also, the visions I receive are usually transparent and fleeting, whereas symbolic landscapes tend to be bright, with sharp vivid colors like a scene from a fairy tale.

Of course, this is the way I see things. For you it might be the opposite. Visions might come into your head in Technicolor and symbols might appear vague and white. Take your time and test for yourself how your psyche functions. Over time you will be able to differentiate between a symbolic picture and a psychic vision just as you are able to tell the difference between a movie and real life. When I am alert and on my toes, my gut tells me what I am seeing. Listen to your instincts. They never lie.

◎ Interpreting Symbols

One of the best ways to interpret a symbol is just to look at it. Symbols are not meant to be intellectually defined. They are meant to be felt, absorbed through the senses like a fine piece of art. If you have a recurring symbol from a dream that intrigues you, or one that keeps popping into your mind, find a way to externalize the symbol through painting, photography, or drawing, and then just sit in a chair and stare at it, letting the symbol inform you of its hidden meaning.

If a symbol just flashes through your mind and you don't have time to sketch it out, take the first thought that comes into your awareness. For instance, if you are thinking about your wife and you see the symbol of a fish in your head, ask yourself what the fish represents and then go with the first idea you receive.

The fish might tell you that your wife is lonely, that she is waterlogged with emotion and needs more of your attention. Or the fish might indicate that you should go swimming together, that the ocean is beckoning your naked bodies!

As a psychic, I have learned to trust the first idea that lights up my brain. Out intuition is an advanced power. When it sends us something, we should go with it, take it all the way to the source. Interpreting symbols is like taking photographs of falling stars. You have to be quick, agile, willing to go beyond your usual thought patterns to receive unexpected brilliance.

Just a second ago I asked my soul for a symbol to guide me through the rest of this chapter. The picture that came into my mind was that of a white Persian cat with a mischievous smile, curled up, sleeping in the air. My immediate association was to play. The symbol made me want to lighten up, to work less hard to make sense out of a subject that was innately mysterious.

The fact that the cat is floating means to me that symbols are a gateway to higher thinking, that when we reach for a symbol, we are reaching for God, for something beyond our understanding, something our mind can never fully interpret.

The symbol also informs me that we are fed by the images in our unconscious mind even when we do nothing with them. Just asking for a symbol and watching it hang there in your mind shifts the energy in your body and takes you on a new course of thought. Your awareness changes. You become something different.

Since I have thought of the cat, my cells are tuned into a new music, and consequently my writing is affected. The hovering feline has opened me to a lighter frequency. I can move into the next moment of writing with less resistance.

◎ Soul Portraits

A few years ago in meditation, I had a vision of myself sitting by a purple lake, with legs like a goat and horns sticking out of my head. I was happy in the vision, feeling connected to nature in a surreal, mythological way. I decided at that moment that I would return to this vision every now and then to see if it changed. I realized instinctually that this picture I was seeing was a soul portrait, an inner mirror which reflected how I was truly feeling.

When I consulted the vision again a few weeks later, I was sitting in a chair wearing a black suit. My body was no longer part goat, and the lake was now clear and ordinary. Since the first time I had observed the portrait, I had been spending less time outdoors and most of my time at home writing a book. The portrait revealed this change. It showed me in a new context, with new attributes to reflect my soul.

Since then I have checked up on this vision at least a hundred times. The portrait has always been reliable and given me clear feedback into my real condition. It is as though I have created a Tarot card inside my body that I may look at to diagnose my life. It enables me to know what is going on without having to ask other people. I can be my own psychic, my own oracle.

If this ritual resonates with you, create your own soul portrait and refer to it for guidance. Ask your soul to show you a picture of how you are doing and then interpret it symbolically with the first idea that comes to your mind.

It is easy for us to lose touch with what is really going on inside us when the surface of our lives remains neutral. The soul portrait will act as a reference point, a mirror for your inner condition. Trust what you see, and remember, symbols often speak to us through exaggerated details. In my own soul portrait I have seen myself decapitated, wearing a straitjacket, naked, made of silver. The symbolic world is the world of myth, where everything is amplified and extreme. If you see something strange in your vision that you don't understand, don't jump the gun. Something that looks negative at first could on a symbolic level represent some sort of breakthrough or positive change.

Take your time with the interpretation. After a while it will get easier to understand what each portrait means. The shaman will take you beyond your rational thinking, and the pathway between you and your soul will get more and more clear.

Learning how to do this exercise will prepare you for reading other oracles, teach you how to be guided by symbols in your everyday life. This very second my soul portrait shows me as a naked child with tree branches growing out of my limbs, standing by a clear lake. What do you think this represents? Look at your own soul portrait right now. Let it speak to you and tell you where you are.

This world is filled with symbols that reflect the depth and complexity of our soul. A flower, a bird, a football game: each of these is symbolic of some underlying pattern that holds us all together.

Learn how to pick out symbols in your daily life. Be open to when your soul is telling you something through a pattern of events that have symbolic meaning. Be mindful of the animals that cross your path, the colors you are drawn to, the foods.

If you learn to trust that your soul is present in the small moments, then you will feel guided all the time. In your darkest hour, there will be a message coming through, a symbol that can lead you home. Be awake. Walk with the eyes of the shaman and everything will fall into place.

Oracles

Be wary of gypsies who ask for big tipsies.
—DR. HUBERT

 Oracles have been around since the beginning of time. Shamans have always devised ways to predict the future by using such articles as stones, cards, and tea leaves. The Egyptians, the Greeks, the Chinese, each culture has its own methods of fortune-telling that date back thousands of years. Some mystics read your life by throwing a handful of bones onto a piece of velvet; others stare into crystal balls or draw esoteric diagrams on paper to diagnose your past lives.

In the late twentieth century, a lot of these rituals are no longer taken seriously. Psychics who use oracles, for the most part, are considered entertainers. The moment someone pulls some Tarot cards or Yarrow sticks out of his bag, the skeptics come out of hiding. This has happened to me many times at parties where I am hired to do readings. When people see me with my cards, they get a sarcastic look on their face. Either that, or they get scared. They think I am a sorcerer, able to cast dark spells, and they move as far away from me as possible.

The truth is, an oracle is whatever you perceive it to be. If you want to turn it into a superstitious device, you can. If you want to keep it rational and grounded, you can do that as well. I always tell my students that they can treat their oracle with respect without being mystified by it. Wrapping your cards in silk, sleeping with your Rune stones under your pillow, placing your *I Ching* on a separate bookshelf; these are fine things to do for ritual's sake, but really an oracle needn't be treated with such fearful care. Your intuitive strength comes from inside you. The oracle is just a tool to activate it. It doesn't hold the power, you do. Eventually you should be able to live without an oracle, to navigate yourself through life by your instincts alone.

There was a man I knew on Venice Beach who turned to his Tarot cards for security as an alcoholic turns to the bottle. Every time someone walked by his table, he would flip through the deck to see if this was a dangerous person. Don't let yourself get this way. Study an oracle, but don't become dependent on it. The voice inside is the one you need to follow. This is where the grace is.

What most people forget when they consult an oracle is that it is an intuitive exercise. They are far too eager to pick up a book and define the card or stone they have drawn rather than letting their instincts tell them what it means. When I learned the Tarot cards, I barely studied the definitions. From the very beginning, I went mostly from my gut. This made me a very good reader in a short time. After a few months, I knew the cards like the back of my hand, and at the same time, I didn't know them at all. They were still full of mystery. Every time I picked them up, they spoke to me with a new voice.

If you work with your oracle spontaneously, you will learn it much more quickly than if you study it formally. Before you take any classes, play around with your cards or stones for a while and see what they teach you. I have had friends with no experience at all give me readings and be stunningly accurate. It's all about intuition. If you listen closely to what you are feeling, you can be a great psychic the first time you try.

After years of doing readings, the cards are now part of my body. I don't just think in thoughts, I think in Tarot images as well. When you find an oracle you like, and use it on a regular basis, the symbols will become part of your thinking. If you are a Rune master, then your thought process will become part Runes. If you read the *I Ching,* then your head will be filled with hexagrams. This is why it is important to find an oracle that inspires you, that has an uplifting tone. Selecting something dark will ultimately have a damaging effect on your life. It would be like reading

Stephen King novels every day. After a while, you're bound to get depressed.

In the next part of the chapter, I am going to list some of the oracles that are available and some different ways you can use them. I suggest you try them all out. Each oracle will awaken a different facet of your psychic awareness. I would even try a crystal ball. It might be the right tool for you; perhaps your gift is clairvoyance. Have fun. See what happens.

If for some reason working with an oracle frightens you, then turn it into an act of play instead. Use your cards or stones with a light heart, a humorous edge. Still if you do not feel comfortable, then stick to the exercises in the book for which you don't need an oracle. Follow your instincts. Do what feels right or don't do it at all.

ⓦ Ouija Boards

Ouija boards are a classic tool of the occult, designed to summon spirits from all dimensions. A Ouija board consists of a flat surface with letters and numbers on it, and a sliding pointer. Placing your hands on the pointer (everyone's hands, if you are not alone), you ask the spirit questions about your life, from why you are here on the planet, to what your future mate will be like. The spirit you are communing with will guide the pointer to the letters and numbers that make up the answer. My sister says that she has been in sessions where the pointer has actually moved on its own, creeping across the board and spelling out words with no one touching it.

Although they are fun to use, Ouija boards tend to attract a lot of lower energy forms, the bottom-feeders of the spirit world. Occasionally you can luck out and hook a sweet angel, but usually this is not the case. For this reason, Ouija boards have never been my favorite oracle. They are too risky. I am not the type of person who likes to interact with ghosts, especially when they are not of the loving kind.

If you absolutely must explore Ouija boards, do some prayer and meditation beforehand to ensure that you only contact benevolent forces. Tell the universe out loud what your intentions are, why it is that you are using the oracle, and whom you wish to communicate with. If during the session you get scared or feel that you need to stop, by all means listen to your intuition. A Ouija board has the power to open doors to other dimensions. If you get a bad feeling about the door you are opening, then put the board away for a while. Do something else. Ask the same question with cards or stones, or consult the *I Ching*.

All in all, Ouija boards are not a wise choice for the beginner psychic. If you are just starting out, wait a while before you try one, a few years at least. After that, if you are still curious, perform a session with a few close friends in a sacred environment. Take what the spirits say with a grain of salt. And if you hook an angel, enjoy it for all it's worth!

◎ Tarot Cards

According to some metaphysical scholars, the first deck of Tarot cards was made by an Italian artist as a present for a princess nearly five hundred years ago. There are other reports that Tarot cards were used much earlier by Persian mystics, to preserve esoteric teachings during times of religious tyranny. Instead of writing in books, the mystics would conceal their insights in symbolic patterns, secret codes that only fellow seekers could understand. For this reason, Tarot cards are generally quite complex in design, as each card is a template of metaphysical knowledge.

It is not surprising to me that the Tarot's origin is mysterious, for the more I use these cards, the more enigmatic they become. I advise that everybody who is wishing to expand their psychic awareness begin by learning to read the Tarot. The Tarot not only refines your intuition, but also teaches you about the cycles of life, the underlying patterns of all human experience. Encoded in the first twenty-two cards is the story of man's journey toward enlightenment, the various leaps and pitfalls that occur when one pursues liberation from worldly struggle.

The more you study the cards, the more of your soul's path will be uncovered. It is partly because of the Tarot that I am writing this book. The cards led me to teaching workshops which eventually became the subject matter for many of the chapters you are reading right now.

Tarot cards have also assisted me in creative realms. When I am writing stories, I use the Tarot to help shape the plot and invent new characters. The Tarot is the tool not just of a shaman, but also of an artist. As I tell my students, whatever it is that you are creating—paintings, sculptures, screenplays, a project at work— the Tarot can offer assistance, give you the extra input you need to work through creative blocks and achieve your vision.

The best way to learn Tarot is just by doing it. When you need a question answered, just sit down, draw a few cards, and let your soul tell you what they mean. Afterward, refer to a guide book for specific insights. The Tarot works well when accompanied by flowing speech, so when you're giving yourself a reading, speak aloud rather than in your head and the cards will have more power.

Also, when you begin the Tarot, reduce your deck in size to ten or fifteen cards, and each day place one of them on your bathroom mirror, letting it be absorbed into your mind subliminally as you shave or put on your makeup. This way each time you draw the card, you will know what it means without thinking. It will be inside you, part of your awareness. Once you have these first cards memorized, you can add more from the rest of the deck, until you have worked your way up to an entire set of cards.

I have had the same deck of medieval Tarot cards for three years and they have been nothing but a source of joy and magic. They are old and worn and smooth to touch. My clients love them. The ornate imagery and gold coloring makes anyone who is read by them feel like he is partaking in an ancient ceremony. When I hold these cards in my hand, time stops. I am a wiser person. The light of my soul is brighter than ever.

When you go out and buy your own deck, take your time. Look around until you find something that really moves you. And then dive right in. Don't worry about spreads or definitions. Just be whimsical and read the cards. Take this from a professional: The Tarot will teach you as you go along. It will lead you deep into your heart where all the answers lie. You just have to trust and let go. The magic will happen on its own.

◎ The *I Ching*

The *I Ching* is one of the oldest books in the world. People have been consulting its wisdom for over four thousand years. It consists of sixty-four small chapters (otherwise known as hexagrams), each of which prescribes a particular style of action to deal with prevailing changes. Usually the advice one gets from the *I*

Ching is simple and direct. *Move. Slow down. Retreat. Advance.* The *I Ching* teaches you how to do less and have more happen, how to give in to the forces of life and be carried like a fish in the sea.

The *I Ching* is not to be read hastily. It is a ritual, not a slot machine. To determine which hexagram you should follow, you must either toss coins or select Yarrow sticks, a process that takes at least twenty minutes to complete. There are many times I have approached the *I Ching* with impatience and received ridiculous answers. The *I Ching* demands that you approach it with the same mindful care as you would approach a tea ceremony. The book teaches you to breathe, to slow down and take your time making decisions.

Learning the *I Ching* is easy. The rules are straightforward and simple to understand. The only problem you might have is finding a translation that pleases you. Some translations of the *I Ching* are quite obtuse. You ask a question about your lover and the book tells you about thunder in a mountain. Of course, the metaphors can be interpreted, but it is nice to have something more concrete to go on, something a Western mind can grasp more easily. If you are looking for a good translation to start with, try getting the one by Alfred Douglas. His version will act as a wonderful introduction to the *I Ching*.

When you find the right book, the *I Ching* is a real jewel of wisdom. It is one of the few oracles that gives its advice clearly, without compromise, enabling you to take a stand and cut through any illusions that might be holding you back.

Carl Jung, one of the forefathers of modern psychology, used the *I Ching* extensively throughout his life. He was often flabbergasted by how accurately it answered his questions. Maybe the legend is right; maybe a great wise being does live within the pages of the book. That is what the mystics say anyhow.

ⓞ Runes

The Runes consist of twenty-four stones, each carrying a letter from the Runic alphabet, which has its origins in Latin and Etruscan culture. They have been around for about two thousand years, serving as a reliable oracle for many of the nomadic tribes of Northern Europe. Ralph Blum, a historian and mystic, has done a wonderful translation of the Runes.

The Runes are tactile. You can hold them in your hand, touch them, feel their heat. When you pick up a Rune stone, it is no longer the twentieth century. You are back in the forest sitting around a fire with stars above your head. Rune means "a secret" or "mystery," and this is the atmosphere they invoke. When you use Runes, you are brought to the core of yourself, the inner chamber where all the answers ring heavy with truth.

Using the Runes is very simple. You just reach your hand into the Rune bag, select a stone, and then interpret it with your intuition. You can do one, two, or three stone readings, depending on how many questions you have. Much like the *I Ching,* the Runes do not give elaborate messages. They speak in simple phrases that give you just the right amount of guidance you need. The symbols of the Runes have been found all over the Western world, even in the United States, carved on stone walls, in caves, on tree stumps. It is my belief that the Rune symbols were floating through our unconscious mind long before they appeared in the visible world. When my mother does her deep trance readings, she sees Rune symbols all the time. They are part of our body, part of our DNA.

I feel the Runes calling me. As I write this section, I have the feeling that one day they will become one of my loyal oracles. If the Runes are calling you, go out and buy a set and study them by reading each stone intuitively before you refer to the guide book. This is how Ralph Blum did his first translation. He touched the Runes and let them speak to his heart. This is the best way to learn any oracle.

As I was writing this chapter, a good friend of mine named John Hoff passed away. He was seventy years old. He had a heart attack alone in his apartment as he was opening one of his closets to put something away. Aside from being my friend, he was also my mother's lover of nine years. It was a tragic day when he left us. We were all speechless with grief.

At the exact moment he died, my mother was walking home with her dog, and a giant raven—John's favorite bird—swooped down above her head, cawed three times in the shrillest voice, then landed on a branch down the street. When my mother heard of his death an hour later, she remembered the raven. It had been a messenger, an oracle sent by God to speak the news of John's departure.

Later that night a friend of my sister's—also named John—called and invited her to the "Raven's Flight" café to listen to some Celtic storytellers. When we heard the name of the café, we all made the connection. It was another sign, another message from the Great Beyond.

I was reminded by these events that the whole world is an oracle. If we are watchful, we can be given readings all the time. Cards, stones, the *I Ching*, Ouija boards—the power invested in these tools exists in all of creation. If you want to make an oracle out of bird feathers or seashells, it will be just as accurate and powerful as something you buy in a metaphysical shop. Prepare it with a shaman's reverence for all things sacred. Use your imagination and follow your intuition. Those are the two key messages of this book. And be watchful during times of crisis for how the world is speaking to you. Hear the raven's call. This is the path of the Shaman.

Psychometry

"Matter is nothing but condensed light."

 Everything we touch has a life story: a rock, a chair, a piece of jewelry. Matter is as much alive as we are, only it thinks differently. We have a mind, and matter has consciousness, or what the Buddhists call beingness. Just as our brain stores information, so does matter. It stores not only its own experiences, but everything it comes in contact with. If a deer licks a stone, then the stone is part deer. If a woman wears a diamond necklace for five years, then the necklace is part woman.

Psychometry is the art of reading the stories contained in matter; not the surface stories, but the soul stories. The surface story of a table would include the type of wood it was made with and where it was built. The soul story would include the people who have sat around the table, where the table has been, and what it has experienced.

Since matter is always moving and changing, the soul story of an object is always in flux. If a watch switches owners, then the energy of the watch will change. The personality of the old owner will slowly wear off and the new owner's personality will become the predominant force the watch is carrying.

Psychometry is one of the oldest shamanistic arts. It is a form of psychic reading that is more about feeling than interpretation. Psychometry is much the same as tasting a sauce with a blindfold on and telling the cook what you are eating, or dipping your hand into a jar of honey and describing the substance with words. In psychometry, the contact is immediate. The less your mind is in the way, the more accurate the reading will be.

A client told me that she went to a psychic's house for a workshop and the psychic invited the entire class to go into the garden, pick a flower, and lay it on the kitchen table while she was waiting in the other room. When they were finished, she then read the flowers one by one, revealing to the students specific facts about their life. The lady was a master at psychometry, able to diagnose a person's character from holding something they had only touched for a few minutes.

This story goes to prove how porous everything is. If a flower can absorb the blueprint of someone's life in a few minutes, then think of what we can absorb from another person we live with and sleep with for twenty years. It's wild to imagine . . .

You can perform psychometry on anything you want—books, chairs, old coins, fruit. In the next part of this chapter, I will explain some specific methods you can apply for various articles, and how to prepare your body to receive psychic information. Again, if any techniques come to you that I fail to mention, try them out. Follow your instincts at all times.

⊚ Preparing the Body

Before you practice psychometry, it is good to clear the body, get your cells focused on the matter at hand. Sit or stand somewhere and allow yourself a few minutes of quiet breathing. At the same time, hang your hands by your side and imagine all the tension that is floating through your body slowly draining to the ends of your fingers.

Then, once you start to feel your hands getting heavy, shake them out. This will scatter the negative energy you are carrying and give you more space in your body to interpret the article you want to read.

You are now ready to do a psychometric reading. Whatever it

is that you want to read, just pick it up in either hand, grasp it gently, and begin tracking your impressions.

◎ Reading Jewelry

Jewelry is the easiest article to read. It stays close to the body, and is therefore a sponge for all the feelings and emotions of the person wearing it. Even long after someone dies, jewelry can still carry the essence of its former owner, evoking memories and sensations in whoever touches it.

I suggest you start reading other people's jewelry rather than your own. It is difficult to be objective with yourself. Borrow an aunt's ring or a war medal from your grandfather, and let yourself fall into its story. Reading your best friend's watch will not be as exciting as reading the watch of someone you just met in a café. Make the experience challenging. Step into the unknown.

If no one around you will volunteer their jewelry for analysis, practice on rings and bracelets at a secondhand shop. Be like Sherlock Holmes. Sniff around. Use your intuition to solve the riddle of everything you touch.

When you are reading a piece of jewelry, numerous things might occur. A few whole scenes might flash into your head, or just a color or a symbol. Your body might all of a sudden get very warm or cold. You might even feel the owner of the jewelry moving inside you, with all their strengths, weaknesses, and limitations.

How you receive the information will be personal. If you wish, talk it over with a friend, and then give him the jewelry and compare your findings. This way you'll be more relaxed, more open to surprise insights.

A few more suggestions . . .

If you meet a married couple, try holding each of their rings and describe their marriage from both points of view, as a kind of party game. You could also have a friend bring you a piece of jewelry from someone you haven't met before, so that you can get some feedback and test your accuracy.

Reading jewelry can also be helpful when you want to know what type of stone or crystal to buy for yourself, or which ring best suits your character. The jewelry we wear should reflect more than just our bank account. Wearing precious metals against our skin affects our energy, our moods, and our behavior. When you select what feels right through touch, you are more likely to purchase something that is in harmony with your body, and healthy for you to wear.

My wife chose a seventy-five-dollar engagement ring for herself because she liked the stone and it felt good on her hand. I knew right then she was a woman who cared about quality and not prestige. Listen to your heart when you hold a piece of jewelry. It will tell you everything you need to know.

⊚ Books

There are two ways to read a book. You can read the words or you can read the spirit of the book. Sometimes I perform the latter when I am browsing in a bookstore. I place my palms flat on the front and back cover and let myself feel what the book is about. I don't try to discern what the story line is, but rather how the book was written, how much heart the author has, how much he cares about what he is writing.

There are few writers who are soulfully engaged with their work. A lot of authors put down words with the same cerebral angst they experienced in college. When I pick up one of these books, it feels as though I am holding a tightly wrapped spring, that the book is more mind than soul. When I open the book and read a few pages, usually my assessment is accurate. The style and content match the feeling I had when I was holding the book in my hands.

I like to be nourished by what I read. Unless I am reading a book on how to fix my blender, I want the writer to be awake and conscious of what he is saying. Taking somebody else's ideas and philosophies into your body can be as intimate as a blood transfusion. Once the ideas are inside you, they have the power to affect the way you think, motivating you to behave in ways contrary to your character. You can avoid this by reading a book through touch first, by examining the writer's integrity through the cells of your body.

If you are really sensitive, you might even be able to figure out what the book is about simply by holding it in your hands. You might receive the image of a battlefield in your head, and soldiers dying, and when you open the book, realize it is a story about World War II. Our bodies are like computer scanners. Just by touching something we absorb information. There have been numerous reports of people falling asleep with books on their chest and assimilating ideas right through their skin. Our whole bodies are psychic, from our head right down to our toes.

You can also perform this ritual with a videocassette. You can hold it flat between your palms, close your eyes, and feel the spirit of the film you are about to rent. If anything, psychometry will refine your intuition, give you evidence of the discriminating powers that dwell inside your body, which could lead you to a more balanced life.

Every minute we have on this planet is precious. Knowing ahead of time the essence of what we are going to read or watch is a way of taking care of ourselves. We are impressionable creatures. The more we choose quality material that feeds our soul, the more peaceful we will be.

◎ Photographs

In his book *Being Peace,* Buddhist monk Thich Nhat Hahn talks about his time translating applications to find sponsors in Europe for Vietnamese orphans. Rather than doing direct translations, he would take thirty or forty seconds to stare at each photo and become one with the child. "Looking at his face or her face," says Hahn, "I got motivated, and I became him and he became me, and together we did the translation."

Upon reading this, I was astonished to find that someone who has never once called himself psychic, or even intuitive, used psychometry in such a natural way. When a client brings me a photograph to read, I do exactly what Thich Nhat Hahn did. I become one with the picture. I let myself dissolve into the person's image and then speak from inside it.

Photographs are easy to do this with, because they are a moment of real life on paper. In one frame, you can see all of a person's character, past, present, and future, like a holograph, staring back at you. Try this with a photograph sometime. Whether it be an author's face on the back of a book, or a movie star in a magazine, just let go of your thoughts and stare into the picture until you uncover the person's soul. If you get stuck, ask yourself some questions along the way. Could I trust this person? Is she happy? Does she like kids? What is she afraid of?

Speak or write down what you see. If you focus for a long time, the person's face will start to change and you will notice she is many people in one, as vast as the night sky.

Perform this exercise with a photograph your friend gives you of someone you have never met before, and let him give you feedback. Do it as a kind of game with your family albums, going back and forth reading people and discussing your impressions.

If someone in your family is dead, place his photograph next to someone who is still alive, and compare the energy. My mother says photographs of people who have died lose light, and gain a historical feeling that is obvious to a sensitive eye. See if you can tell the difference.

Reading photographs can be a great way to get to know somebody on a deeper level, especially if you have access to photographs from early periods of their life, when they were still growing and maturing. Seeing someone in these stages will open your awareness, help you understand why they have become the person they are and where they are going.

Sometimes when I am in a fight with my wife, I call forth in my memory a certain picture of her as a five-year-old girl standing on her front lawn in a snowsuit. Seeing this picture helps me love her all over again, and let go of whatever silly thing we are squabbling about.

Photographs help us see through time. They are gateways to the soul. If you want to really know someone on a deep level, get a picture of him and meditate on it. You will find out everything you need to know, and more. He will be easier to love, because you have seen through his masks and into his heart. Once you get this far, it is easy to care for anyone.

When we touch something, not only are we opening ourselves to receive information, we are also sending love into the object, cherishing it, making it feel good. For this reason, it is good to touch your food before you cook it, to spend a few minutes holding an apple before you put it into your mouth as a way of welcoming it into your body.

Through our sense of touch, we are all great healers. It has been proven that plants whose leaves are stroked and caressed live longer, healthier lives. Even a piece of furniture, when it is cared for, polished, treated with love and respect, has a happier presence in the corner of the room.

On an atomic level, everything in the universe is alive. When we acknowledge this life force through touch, our field of awareness expands. Suddenly we are in league not only with humans and animals, but with everything around us. The whole world becomes our body. This is what the Buddhists believe, that the forest is our lungs, the rivers our blood. Psychometry helps us bridge this gap, to achieve a stronger union with all sentient beings, from ants, to whales, to a piece of wood.

A friend of mine performs psychometry on people's bodies. She is a masseuse and healer, and is able to tell you the story of your life by touching your body. She was working on my back one day and said to me, "Who is this?" Her hand was pressing on a knot in my shoulder. Without thinking, I said, "It is my father." Something in her knew that the pain I was carrying was not just my own, that it was someone else's sorrow I had taken on unconsciously.

Let your hands be messengers to your mind. When you touch your lover, get to know the story of her body. There is a lot we can learn just by laying our hands on another person's skin. Through the pads of your fingers, allow yourself to hear all the silent calls the voice cannot utter. Be awake in your flesh. Let your touch tell you things your eyes cannot see.

Language

In the beginning, there was the word.
—*The Holy Bible*

 Having a soulful grasp of language is an essential part of becoming a psychic. Being intuitive is not enough; you must be able to express yourself in words. There is a magic that happens when a complex feeling or idea is transmuted into language. It's as if the body suddenly understands what it is going through and feels a clear purpose in its existence. When you speak or write soulfully, you connect the fragmented parts of yourself and experience a wonderful sense of inner unity. For a moment you are healed. You break through the confusion to a place of shining insight.

Being able to communicate what exists in your heart gives you a recognizable identity, something solid to hold on to. More than anything, this is what we are all searching for. We long to feel intimate with ourselves, to be in tune with the specific instincts that make us who we are. Words can help us do this.

If you study the lives of dedicated writers, you will notice how over the years their language evolves, pushing them deeper and deeper into themselves, until they expose a voice that is uniquely their own. Each time they sit down to write, they are giving themselves hard-core therapy, a three- or four-hour psychic reading.

Their muses help them chisel away at what is false, at the conditioned parts of their psyche that guard the masterpiece.

If you wish to fulfill your dreams, they cannot remain mute. Even if you are not a writer, it is important to develop a relationship with language where each day you are being refined, brought out of your usual speaking habits into a more specific and soulful mode of expression. Unless you are surrounded by poets like Oscar Wilde, it is difficult to achieve this discipline through conversation. You must learn to write, to help the muddled sounds of your dreams become a clear song.

In my workshops, this is one of the first things I teach. I give my students a series of writing exercises designed to access the psychic mind, and at the same time help them find their authentic voice. A lot of people aren't used to speaking from a place of intuition and feeling. When they talk of their inner life, they tend to use a metaphysical vocabulary that usually has nothing to do with what is really going on. I used to be one of those people. I so feared the consequences of being honest, that people didn't understand what I was saying. I was about as straightforward as a boomerang. I said the word "spiritual" every third sentence. It is much harder to be honest and use words that mean something than it is to speak of angels and fairies. For me this has been a recurring lesson, something I am still working on every day.

Every person is born with a different voice, a different way of organizing words into speech. My belief is that the more you return to your natural language, the more psychic you become. The shaman says things as the soul sees them rather than just reporting the subjective opinions of his mind. The soul is anchored in the fire of life itself. It is humorous, daring, unpredictable. Let it do the talking. Just get out of the way. It knows what to say. When the soul is invited to speak, the speaker should listen as well.

The following exercise will help you develop this capacity. Not only will it enhance your ability to express what your psychic mind observes, but it will also open the doorway to deeper perceptions, visions of future and past that are otherwise locked away. I call them stream-of-consciousness portraits. Here's how they work.

First of all, choose one of two people to write about: either your mother or your father. It doesn't matter whom you do first; eventually you should do the exercise with both. Personally, I think it's a good idea to start with your mother. That's where you came from. She was your first home, the first person who held and fed you. If you start with your mother, it should lead to your father quite nicely.

For those of you who were adopted, the exercise will be equally effective. However, I do suggest that after you have done it with your adoptive parents, you try it with your biological parents as well. Even though they didn't raise you, the memory of them is in your cells. There might be some interesting material there. The wall between you and your past might not be as thick as you think.

The reason I start the exercise with parents is that I have discovered in my workshops that few people see their parents objectively. No matter how old they are, they tend to see Mom and Dad through five-year-old eyes. Until we really understand where we came from, it is impossible for us to move into our own individual existence. It's a hard circle to break, but if we don't, our culture will always wear diapers.

When we enter into our parents' psyches, we are opening ourselves to a genetic continuum from which we can draw a lot of information. We start to hear the breath of our ancestors, see our past lives, understand the origin of our dreams and ambitions.

Our parents are an important step in our soul's history, the bridge that connects us to the human stream. When we examine the material of their lives, we see ourselves reflected in it. Sometimes it feels as if it is they who are looking for us, that we are the result of the questions they asked but were never able to answer. The past is like a holograph. We are the farthest point of a series of overlapping identities. When we heal the issues with our parents—the earliest layer of ourselves—we set ourselves free to discover who and what we really are.

So, on with the exercise . . .

Once you have selected a person, either your mother or your father, take a blank piece of paper and start to write quickly, without thinking. Write fast and furiously every word or phrase that comes to you when you think of that person. Let the words gush out onto the paper. Try to keep things short. Let the words fly out like bullets. One after the other.

Don't get caught with words like "nice" and "tall." Be specific. If you are writing about your mother, describe the perfume she wears, the energy of her walk, a landscape that reminds you of her—the desert, the mountains, the sea, a shopping mall. Write about her emotional patterns, her eyes, her umbrella, her favorite food. Describe the colors that make up her personality: blue, yellow, turquoise, white, black, green.

Whatever comes to you, write it down. An early memory might come up in your mind, perhaps a phrase she always says when she is happy. Don't exclude anything. And be honest. List the good, the bad, and the ugly. Write for at least ten minutes until you feel that you have said everything that you could possibly say about the person. Write until you have captured his or her essence on the page.

Remember, the intention of this exercise is to excite the abstract, nonlinear, psychic part of your brain. When you give an actual reading to someone, it is not going to come out so poetically. When you do a reading orally, for a stranger, it is going to be more like prose, more conversational. You will have less specific information to draw from, because the person will be more of a mystery. But when you are starting as a psychic, it's better to just turn on the faucet and let everything out. Form and structure come later, once you are familiar with the spontaneous nature of your psychic voice.

Remember, no matter how accurate it is, a psychic reading is impressionistic. Just like a writer or a painter, the psychic's mind is in a state of retrieval, catching images and ideas as they appear from the unconscious. The facts come forth from feelings, not the other way around. It is better to make the occasional mistake and remain open in the heart than it is to be strict and surgical and miss the point entirely.

In a psychic reading, the edges are not always sharp. Sometimes things are blurry, only partly formed. Don't worry about it. Omniscience can take a while, a few hundred lives at least . . . What you find is meant to be found, and the rest, well, it's meant to remain hidden, at least for the time being. In some of the best readings I have done, I was only able to solve half the puzzle. The rest the client finished on his own, either during the reading or sometime later on. A psychic reading is a work in progress. Even the slightest clue can help someone change her life. Quality, not quantity, as the old adage goes.

Here's an example of how the exercise might look on paper. As I was writing this chapter, I got a call from an actress in San Francisco for a phone reading. The entire time I was talking to her, I kept seeing the color blue around her. It just hovered there in my mind's eye for the whole reading. The more I allowed myself to feel the color, to let it speak through me, the more accurate the reading became. For months, my client had been trapped in a heavy melancholy mood. She wanted to know what was going on, and how to get rid of it. The reading revealed that this sadness she was feeling was a good thing. It was forcing her to go into herself to a depth she had never explored. She couldn't get there with joy. She needed a heavier feeling to sink to that place in herself where her soul wanted to go.

Here is the stream of consciousness portrait that came to me at the end of her reading, after I had been exposed to her for thirty minutes of conversation.

> *woman still feeling like a girl lost no daddy around holding something something that means something to her what is she holding something white her innocence afraid of dying of growing up lost innocence man beside her tall ivy league kind of guy can't tell him what she really feels horses riding horses and eating sweet foods in her warm blue room little girl little girl shy where am I where am i where am i the future is a dark movie world big bad monster in the closet of my ambition fear mistrust lost little girl life turning wild travel future live to be very old one day return to the motherhood happy and in another career trees in backyard smell of blossoms living with new man . . .*

Now do yours. As you can see, mine just rambles on, like rain on a roof, random, penetrating, whimsical. Don't punctuate. Let the words bleed together. Go ahead. Give it a try.

After you are finished writing, take a deep breath and close your eyes for a few minutes. Let the images and sensations that the exercise has brought up circle around in you for a bit. See if you can identify which parts of your parent you love and which parts you are ashamed of. Are there certain parts of your body where you carry these feelings? Your shoulders, your jaw, your stomach? If so, you can do the stream-of-consciousness exercise again on the specific part of your body that is carrying these feelings. It might have its own voice, an important message for you about what it needs to heal itself.

As Deepak Chopra has informed us, each part of the body has its own personality; and a healthy body is the result of a flowing dialogue among all these parts. This exercise has the power to illuminate problems that exist on an energetic level before they manifest in the body. Writing like this engages our subconscious mind and can act as preventative medicine. So when you come back from the meditation, write the information down for future reference. It is always good to know where the body needs healing. You can take the information to your masseuse or a holistic doctor. These people are aware of such matters, and can provide you with remedies that will help you dissolve the problem before it shows up as an illness later on. Sometimes all it takes are a few good massages to bring everything into movement. When treated well, the body responds very quickly.

This exercise gives proof that the people we love don't just live outside of us. They also exist inside our bodies. By acknowledging their presence, we eliminate the unconscious influence they have on our will, which in turn gives us more freedom to pursue our soul's path.

After doing this exercise, it is most likely that you will feel a whole series of contradictory moods: happy, sad, puzzled, angry. Whenever we dig deeply into ourselves, it is almost inevitable that we encounter confusion, paradoxes, things that just don't make sense. Whatever you are feeling, write it all down and put a date on the page. You can do the exercise again in a few months to see how things have changed. For now, embrace the confusion. After the dust settles, your vision will be much clearer than before.

When you are ready, return your attention to the words you have written. Read over them a few times. If certain words or phrases stand out as particularly accurate, underline them. Specify in what way they are accurate. Is it because the words are playful that they are accurate, because they are loving and compassionate, or is it because they sting like arrows of truth? It is important to study the words so that you can get an understanding of how it is that you best express yourself, whether your voice is a humorous one, or whether the way you describe things is more serious and forthright.

The more you do this exercise, the more rounded your voice will become. I tend to gravitate to a foolish voice a lot, a kind of adolescent jester who loves to make jokes at the expense of the sacred. After a lot of work, I have finally come to the point where this voice works for me rather than against me. I am very firm with it now. I tell it that it is allowed to speak only when it is absolutely necessary, that its powers are better received in moderation than they are in abundance.

Another way of expanding your voice is to set intentions before you do the exercise. Take a second before you write about your next subject to quietly tell your soul how you want to express yourself. This will influence the flow of words that comes out of you. Setting an intention gives order to the higher powers, calls forth whatever energy you need to fulfill your task. For example, if you are accurate only in the praiseworthy words, then you might set the intention to be less flattering, to let your mind see the whole picture, warts and all. Or if you have no sense of humor, can only see things through the gray eyes of seriousness, you can set the intention to see the funny side of everything, allowing the Immortal Jester to lighten your words.

As a psychic, it is important to have access to a wide range of expression. From my years of psychic work, I have discovered that the reason most of us have difficulty achieving our dreams is that we have been conditioned to express only a very small part of our character. At some point in our lives we were so brutally defined by those around us that we cut off vital parts of ourselves in exchange for love and acceptance.

By the time we are adults, most of us have been so pared away, that when we set out to accomplish our dreams, we realize that we are missing certain qualities needed to fulfill the task. We are like a car with three wheels, spinning in circles and never reaching our destination. In order to remain loyal to our soul's path, we have to keep plunging into our subconscious to recover the parts of us that have been lost and damaged by time. This is not easy; it takes work and patience, and a lot of self love.

Personally, I have found writing to be an amazing tool of exploration. Each time I do this exercise, some new part of me is excavated, carried up from the shadows for all to see. For many, it is the psychic part of us that has been buried away and needs to be revived. Against society's constant praise of logic and reason, our intuitive nature can easily disappear into the underworld. A metaphor I like to use is that of a hiker dropping his compass in the woods. Without the psychic part of us intact, our lives begin to feel like a dense wilderness with no way out. We need to bend down into the shadows and retrieve this valuable instrument. With it, we will start to see our way, and make our journey into the part of the world where we belong.

The next step of the exercise is for those who wish to express their psychic ability through an oracle such as Tarot cards or Runes. If you are not one of these people, then you can just read through this until you get to the next part of the exercise. Personally, I think it's a good idea to have access to an oracle, even if it's something you invent, perhaps a series of colored stones or hand-drawn pictures. The oracle acts as a witness. It guides the flow of information into tangible messages, dividing a whole rush of energy into communicable sections. A lot of the time our brains are too fired up to hear what our soul wants to tell us. An oracle is like an interpreter. It translates messages for us that the static of our thinking prevents us from hearing.

Now as you look at the page of words you have written, go through your deck of cards (or whatever oracle you are using) and select two or three that seem to represent what you have written. For example, if you wrote words like "lonely" and "isolated" and "out of reach," you might choose the Hermit Card or the Rune of Separation.

Select cards that carry the energy of the person you described rather than just their superficial features. This will help you make better predictions, for the farther you travel into someone's character, the easier it is to identify where he is going and where he came from. When you see a person at his core, it is like seeing a wave of sound moving through the air or a leaf growing. His destination is part of his identity. The two are woven together.

After you have matched up the words and phrases, put the page of words away for a while and concentrate on your oracle. Lay them in front of you and stare at them until you can feel the energy of the person you described lurking within them.

An oracle is like a series of computer disks. The more they are used, the more information gets stored inside them. When you start off, they are empty, generic, lifeless. But once you start imbuing them with your own words and impressions, they start to become part of your body, an extension of your psychic mind.

Of course, the symbols found in the oracles are as ancient as

Moses himself, and carry within them millennia of wisdom, but until they are activated by your own soul's experience, they are merely artifacts, unable to reflect the unfathomable insights that live within you.

Doing the writing exercise gives the oracle a new clarity. It connects the symbols to your own language. The more you are able to see your own words and feelings in the images of the oracle, the more your mind will be able to produce the images on its own. After doing as many readings as I have, my mind is able to call forth images without any external device—and I can use a new deck of cards as if they had been with me for years. In some readings the words come out of my mouth at the same time the card lands on the table. They are interconnected, like the adjacent pages of an art book, with the picture on one page and the words describing it on the other.

As an analyst friend of mine said, "In order to read an oracle well, you must be able to perceive at least twenty meanings in each card or stone, otherwise you are speaking from judgment rather than insight. Before an oracle has any value, it must be connected to the reader. Until then it is just like a horoscope in a magazine . . . skin deep . . ."

The final part of the exercise is to read the page of words aloud to yourself three or four times, until it feels as though it is coming from your heart, from the very center of your being. Read it slowly, and as you read it, think to yourself, "I am now doing a psychic reading. These words, these impressions that I have mined from my soul, are real. They have value. This is the way my spirit speaks."

The more often you do this exercise, the sharper your talents will become. Once you have done it with your parents, you can do it on yourself, with your friends, lovers, pets. You can also do the exercise for your oracle, writing about each card or stone as if it were a person you had just met on the street. This keeps the oracles from getting static, keeps them fresh and responsive.

If you have trouble with someone at work, at the end of the day you can do a stream-of-consciousness portrait as a method of personal therapy. The subconscious mind often gives much better advice than ordinary thinking. You might find out that a part of you actually likes your boss, that you are actually attracted to his stubborn and arrogant mind.

Personally, I find this writing exercise to be the most accurate method of self-reading that I have come across. When you read the cards for yourself or pick through the Rune bag, there is too much time for interpretation. But when you write out the messages by hand, from soul to paper, there is little time to sculpt a desired response. The answers appear spontaneously, with no time for self-deception.

People always ask me, "What does it feel like when you are giving a reading? How does it work?"

Well, this exercise is the answer. While you were writing, that moment when you felt connected to your parents' souls, to who they really are, is exactly the same feeling I get when I am involved with a client. A psychic reading is an artistic experience. In some of my readings I feel more like a painter than a metaphysician. Each word I say is like the stroke of a paintbrush, showing a different color, a different shade of who the person is.

Unfortunately our present society doesn't have the same respect for words that it used to. If we don't watch out, our sense of language will continue to deteriorate, and Shakespeare will be reduced to thirty-second sound bites on MTV. As a poet friend of mine said, until something is put into words, it isn't real. That's why American culture can so easily go into denial. It fails to honor the soul's language.

The more people allow their own intuition to be spoken, the more honest things will get. I have a feeling that in twenty years it will be quite common for people to have their psychic voice active in day-to-day life, to meet someone at a business lunch who freely gives you a psychic message before heading back to the office.

Can you imagine that? What a fun world that would be.

I have learned from my psychic work that the mysteries of human behavior are only temporarily unexplainable. If we keep pursuing that which is unknown to us, one day we will be able to uncover what it is. The more trust we put in the language of the soul, the more it will serve us. Our lives are not beyond description. If we go to the essence of things, we can become intimate with the mystery of our own being.

Humor

Excess of sorrow laughs. Excess of joy weeps.
—WILLIAM BLAKE

 One night in Hollywood a client asked me if she was going to have a relationship with a famous movie star she liked. She had never met the person before, but felt they had some kind of connection, that their meeting was meant to be. When I asked her for the star's name, she said she didn't want to tell me, that she would rather I just read the cards.

I smiled and said, "Who is it, Johnny Depp?" The words just slipped out of my mouth, without thought.

The woman jumped in her chair. "How did you know?" she said. "How did you know?"

This kind of thing happens to me all the time. I'll say something as a joke and it turns out to be right on the money. On another occasion I said to a client, "Pick the cards now, Sparky." It turned out that Sparky was the nickname she called her car. Did I know this when I said it? Of course not. The comment just appeared out of the blue, like a scene in a pop-up book. I, too, was surprised, and charmed by the hidden dimension.

Other than jokes we plan ahead of time, humor can be a great vehicle for intuitive thought. Humor helps us tap into another level of thinking, to give voice to spontaneous ideas that would otherwise stay trapped in our head. For this reason, I always allow room in my readings for play, for absurd, whimsical comments. This way I don't block the good stuff from coming through, the unexpected jewels. Artists such as Robin Williams and novelist Richard Brautigan have taught me this. From them I have learned that the gods often say their best lines in the form of comedy, that next to a singer, a humorist is the most capable of translating the holy word.

So when something funny wants to slip through you, say it. Don't live life in a state of rehearsal. Let the unexpected flow out of you. A good shaman allows the "trickster" energy to instruct him and often does his best work while improvising. Like a jazz musician, he is most capable of spitting out a pearl accidentally, as a kind of spontaneous blessing. You can't practice for this; you just have to be open, willing to step outside your persona and become something new.

There is an old saying that the devil never laughs at himself. He might tease and mock others, but he is unable to experience self-irony. I have met a lot of psychics like this. They take themselves so seriously they grow horns. The good thing about humor is that it keeps you human, close to the ground. In developing your psychic ability, this is very important. People who don't have a sense of humor and awaken these powers end up calling themselves Zoron the Great or The Seeing Swan. Keep humor as your companion and this won't happen to you. Always be willing to laugh at yourself, because no matter how intuitive you become, you are still just a human being, and capable of misperceiving reality just as much as anyone else.

I've made hundreds of errors and my clients still keep coming back. They trust me because I don't try to be a superhero in their presence. I laugh with them, crack jokes, tell personal stories. Being psychic does not mean being somber. It is a field in which you need a light heart in order not to become jaded. The more I do it, the less pressure I put on myself to be perfect, and the more receptive I am to spontaneous insights. I just say what I see and leave the rest up to fate. Only when I try to be all-knowing do I get into trouble. If I stay humble, and keep humor close by, everything works out fine.

◉ Seeing What Is Real

Children have an amazing talent for sensing when an adult is not being genuine. The old phrase "Out of the mouths of babes" sums up all those marvelous times that a child has blurted out the truth and forced a grown-up to put down his disguise and show his true face.

Growing up, my wife did this all the time. Her childish curiosity led her to imitate people's behavior. She would become a funny mirror, reflecting back to them everything about their personality that was not real. As a psychic, I have learned to do this in a more subtle way. When I feel in my gut that someone is playing a character rather than being himself, I will try to joke him back to his feet.

One night at a party I saw a woman in a long red dress standing like a sad statue in the middle of the room, talking to no one. Somehow she felt this persona was attractive, that it would win her some attention. During her reading, I joked around with her a bit, and told her that the little girl inside her wanted to come out and play. After a few minutes, she got what I was saying. She relaxed in her chair, and became more real and honest. This is the beauty of humor. It can be used to remove a mask, help expose a part of someone's character that is begging to come out.

As my friend Scott says, humor travels at a faster speed than ordinary conversation. Receiving a joke is like catching a butterfly. You need to be swift on your toes, completely in the moment. For this reason humor can disarm people, dipping behind the scenes with the agility of a celebrity photographer, snatching private views that the rational mind misses.

Usually the more truthful I am in a reading, the more my clients laugh. There is a link between honesty and humor that runs very deep. Telling people they have a messy bedroom or that their lover has a hairy back can make them unwind enough to hear the more serious, emotional parts of the reading. Humor for some people is like Valium. It softens their bones, makes them more available to love and affection.

Allowing more humor into your perceptions will give you a clearer sense of when something is off, when somebody is trying to be something they aren't. We live in a world of appearances. Everything has flaws, cracks, shadows. If you let yourself play the fool now and then, your observations will become more intuitive. You will be able to spot a fraud in the blink of an eye.

At a conference I heard the Dalai Lama say that we should examine our spiritual teachers with the curiosity of a dog. We should sniff their behind as well as their front, so that we get the whole picture of who they are. Humor gives us this kind of broad view. It shows us what is hidden and cloaked—the good, the bad, and the ugly of someone's character.

Whenever you feel mistrusting of a person or a situation, let the humorist in you point out the conflicting details, the irony, the contradictions. Don't be afraid to see everything. In the long run, it will make you a more compassionate person. As you start to see other people's secrets, you will see your own. As you start to identify what is false in those around you, you will identify what is false in yourself.

◎ Just Do It

I met a fellow named Kurt who calls himself a psychic comedian. He has some Swedish ancestors who were renowned clairvoyants, and he, too, carries the gift. When he performs live, he says he draws information from behind his head, from a floating palette. With his shining eyes and curly hair, Kurt looks a lot like the Greek god Pan. One expects him to have a hut in the woods and a tribe of nymphs he plays music with. His laugh is sharp and contagious.

On a night I was feeling down, Kurt offered to give me a reading. He had never used Tarot cards before, but felt he could do it. He wasn't nervous at all. Improvisation is his middle name.

Kurt gave me one of the best readings I've ever had. His special blend of humor and honesty made me laugh and cry at the same time. He read the cards one by one, staring into my eyes with warm affection. He slipped from the voice of a sincere forty-year-old-man to a wild talk show host and back again, pulling ideas out of the air like fluorescent pizzas.

Humor is vast. Knowing this part of yourself will give you the confidence to plunge into the moment and not be afraid to make mistakes, to be the shaman and not worry whether or not your hat has stars on it. In developing your psychic ability, it is crucial you have this range, that you are willing to screw up every now and then, to turn into a clown to convey the truth that is stirring in your bones.

After two meetings, Kurt and I became good friends. I wanted to include him in this book because he is the first psychic artist I have met outside my family and close friends. He was a master Tarot reader the first time he tried. This is very much what this book is about: recovering the wisdom of your soul in an instant. Being the shaman: trusting your insights and opening yourself to a life of revelations . . .

⦿ How to Find Dr. Hubert

As you will notice, several times throughout this book I have quoted a man by the name of Dr. Hubert. I'll let you know right now, he is not human. He is part of my imagination. Dr. Hubert is a character I met last year, a goofy metaphysical psychic who lives inside of me. He is the classic nerd. I met him at one of my men's group meetings. We do a lot of comedy skits, and he just showed up one day, speaking through me with a much more nasal voice than my own. He has been with me a long time now, but it is only recently that I have let him out of hiding.

Dr. Hubert wears checks and stripes at the same time, and extra large beige Hush Puppies. His favorite pastime is to sit cross-legged and talk to people in very complicated sentences about whatever comes into his mind. I will let him speak for a moment right now to give you an example of how his brain works.

"The way the world moves is simple. Everyone has a head and everyone has eyes. When the two move together, a lot of good things can happen. When your head moves with your eyes, then your hands can join the party and have a drink with you. Only a few people know how to move their eyes, head, and hands at the same time. When you do this, your feet join the show, and before long, you are walking in truth. But I am still sitting right now. We haven't gotten that far yet . . ."

Okay, Dr. Hubert, thank you. He could go on forever if I let him. He has a lot of interesting things to say that mean a lot and nothing at the same time. I have let him speak through me because this is the exercise I am assigning you . . . Find your own Dr. Hubert, a character that represents the eccentric, humorous, psychic part of you that you don't allow to speak in your life. Figure out what this character wears, how it talks, what its habits are, whether or not it is married.

If you want, dress up as this character for Halloween one year, or write some stories using its voice. Let a fusion take place. In the future I am going to let Dr. Hubert write the self-help book he wants to write called, "Welcome to the Healing Ranch." I know one day we will sit down together and punch this one out.

When you find this character, you will have a new mind to draw from, one that thinks original thoughts, awakens your intuition and pushes you into play. My friend George has a character he plays called The Reverend. He is a Baptist preacher who has converted from Christianity to Hinduism and is looking for a new congregation. He wears a white towel on his head, a sheet around his body, and a green sticker above his eyes which symbolizes his rapid enlightenment. He has a wild philosophical mind that can describe the universe the way a carpenter describes a house. He is also very psychic, often saying things that blow people away.

For me, Dr. Hubert is just the beginning. I feel many more characters stirring inside me, each of them able to communicate another facet of psychic awareness. The more I let them speak, the easier it is for me to be uninhibited in my daily life, in tune with my instincts without any shame or embarrassment.

If you have kids, they will love this exercise. They might even be able to help you find your character. Kids have a way of seeing the funny parts of us better than we do. They go for what is natural rather than what is rehearsed.

P.S. When you are ready, try giving yourself or another person a reading with this character. Speak in the voice that comes to you, or if you are too shy, write it down. Dr. Hubert has given many people some very wise advice. When the moment is appropriate, I let him speak in my readings, giving my clients a few humorous insights for the road.

Being psychic is like navigating by starlight. This character will help you jump from one constellation to the next. Just trust what you find, and don't be afraid to be silly. Every great shaman is also a great fool.

My favorite Chinese philosopher is Chuang-Tsu. He lived five thousand years ago and was famous for his humorous, matter-of-fact truths. Chuang-Tsu never beat around the bush. His ideas left you well fed and laughing about life. Over the years, he has been a teacher for me in the art of living lightly. With his insights, I can travel the world with less effort, and have fun no matter what is going on.

There is a story about Chang-Tsu that says when his wife died, rather than grieving at the funeral, he picked up a salad bowl and began drumming it and singing to the heavens. When his friend asked him what he was doing, he said there was no way of bringing her back, so he just wanted to play music.

There is a part in all of us that is this brave and joyous even in the face of death. Getting to know your own humor, its pitch and flavor, will lead you to this place. Along the way, you'll recover all the intuitive power that the serious, grown-up world has forced you to abandon. Where before you got angry, now you'll be laughing, because you will see the universe at play.

My friend Lorin says that for him humor is about comparison. When two very unalike things come up side by side, it causes him to roar with laughter. That is why being human is so funny. We are these huge powerful souls living in small frail bodies. The more you study us, the funnier we appear. To alien civilizations, we must be like a sit-com.

Trust your humor. It can be a great receiver for psychic truth. Let whiskers grow from the sides of your mouth and pointed ears sprout from your head. Be the playful coyote. It is a wild show, this life, enough to make anyone roll on the floor.

Parting joke:

Q: *What do you get when you cross an agnostic with a Jehovah's Witness?*
A: Someone who knocks on your door and shrugs.

THREE MORE WAYS TO INVOKE THE SHAMAN

1. Create a personal altar somewhere in your house that you use as a contact point between you and your soul. Decorate it with anything that bears a personal spiritual meaning: feathers, photographs, candles, incense. When you wish to be more in touch with the shaman part of yourself, come to this place and meditate. Kneel down on a pillow and let your body converge with the higher forces.

If you want, you can also use the altar as a meeting place for your dead relatives. If you wish to speak with someone who has passed away, address him or her in prayer when you are sitting at your altar. Spirits respond well to ritual. When we do something with formality, it is easier to invoke their presence.

2. Practice hands-on healing with those you love. If someone you care for is in emotional or physical pain, lay your hands on his body and give him a psychic healing. Imagine the light of your soul pouring through the top of your head and out the ends of your fingers. Breathe steadily. When your hands start to heat up, move them to areas of the body that you feel need attention. Usually the heart and the forehead are the two places that need the most care. Follow your instincts. As you will see, psychic healing has a very natural feel to it. The first time you do it, you will feel as if you have done it many times before.

3. Perform a full moon ritual with your friends. Gather together one evening with a handful of stories and rituals and honor the woman of the sky. Shamans have been conducting full moon rituals for thousands of years. They work best if you make them up as you go along. Certain activities that are a must on a full moon night are: storytelling, dancing, and prayer. The moon responds well to these primitive actions. Also, see if you can find a drum. There is nothing like a full moon night filled with the sound of drums. They will definitely wake up your psychic powers, and get you moving like the mystics of old, in and out of the shadowy night.

Conclusion

What the caterpillar calls the end of the world, the master
calls a butterfly.

—RICHARD BACH

 It has been my intention with this book to introduce
you to the psychic world in as lighthearted a manner
as possible. The exercises and rituals I have provided
are meant to be practiced as a kind of sacred play. At
all times I recommend that you go at your own pace, that you
assimilate the material in the book at a speed that feels comfortable
and safe. There is no need to rush your psychic development. If
you need to stay working on one chapter for a long time, then do
so. It is likely that certain facets of psychic awareness will come
more easily than others. I have noticed this with my students. One
person, for example, may find it easy to perceive colors, and another
person may have a more immediate contact with his guides. This
kind of work is very personal, and the results will vary a great deal
from one individual to the next.

Another thing to keep in mind is your spirituality. Now that
you have begun to awaken your psychic instincts, there will be a
greater need for a tangible relationship with your soul. It can be
overwhelming at first to be open to new fields of information, new
dimensions, and a solid spiritual foundation is the best prevention
against any kind of psychic overload. Cultivating a healthy medita-

tion program or learning the art of affirmative prayer can be wonderful tools to keep you in touch with your higher self. Remember,
the veils will come off when they are meant to. There is no need
to rush the process.

I also advise that you select a few friends to keep journeying
with you through the material of the book. Sharing these experiences with other people and having some feedback will make your
psychic discoveries more meaningful. Every time I sit down with
a client, we go traveling together, opening doors, exploring new
vistas. The psychic world is more easily penetrated in a group than
if you are alone. Trust your instincts. Choose individuals who will
not be intimidated by mystical happenings, people whose minds
are open and willing to grow.

As I wrote this book, I encountered many synchronicities, many
chance happenings that affected the direction of my writing and
led me to new insights. Reading this book will also take you into
the same kind of magical flow. Trust the events and people the
book places in your path. As Henry Miller said, a book is a living
organism. Just as much as a tree or an animal, it has its own
intelligence, its own soul. Let the book lead you to new experiences,
new encounters with reality.

Final suggestion: Now that you are finished reading the book,
mark a spot six months ahead on your calendar where you can
come back and read the book again. This way you will be able to
monitor your progress, and determine for yourself how much you
have grown.

I wish you the best of luck on your journey. May the gods bless
and protect you as you uncover the new frontiers of your soul's
path.

For a private consultation with Andrei, please call (310) 280-3554, or you can E-mail him at JossyJos@aol.com if you have any questions that you would like to ask him in regards to his book.